MEMOIRS OF THE IRISH WARS

**THE EARL OF CASTLEHAVEN'S
MEMOIRS OF THE IRISH WARS (1684)**

with

**THE EARL OF ANGLESEY'S
LETTER FROM A PERSON OF HONOUR
IN THE COUNTREY**

FACSIMILE REPRODUCTIONS
WITH AN INTRODUCTION
BY DOUGLAS G. GREENE

SCHOLARS' FACSIMILES & REPRINTS
Delmar, New York, 1974

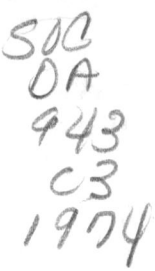

A facsimile re-edition published by
Scholars' Facsimiles & Reprints, Inc.
P.O. Box 344, Delmar, New York 12054

Reproduced with permission from copies in
The Newberry Library, Chicago, Illinois

© 1974 Scholars' Facsimiles & Reprints, Inc.
All rights reserved

Printed in the United States of America

Library of Congress Cataloging in Publication Data

Castlehaven, James Touchet, 3d Earl of, 1617?-1684.
   The Earl of Castlehaven's Memoirs of the Irish Wars (1684).

   Reprint of 2 works, the 1st printed in 1684 for C. Brome, London, under the title: The Earl of Castlehaven's revievv; or, His memoirs of his engagement and carriage in the Irish Wars; the 2d printed in 1681 for N. Ponder, London, under the title: A letter from a person of honour in the countrey written to the Earl of Castlehaven, being observations and reflections upon his Lordships Memoires concerning the Wars of Ireland.
   Includes bibliographical references.
   1. Ireland—History—1625-1649—Sources.
   2. Castlehaven, James Touchet, 3rd Earl of, 1617?-1684.
   3. Anglesey, Arthur Annesley, 1st Earl of, 1614-1686.
   I. Anglesey, Arthur Annesley, 1st Earl of, 1614-1686.
   A letter from a person of honour in the countrey. 1974.
   II. Title.   III. Title: Memoirs of the Irish Wars (1684)
   DA943.C3   1974   941.56'092'2 [B]   74-3345
                  ISBN 0-8201-1128-7

Robert Manning Strozier Library

JAN 27 1975

Tallahassee, Florida

INTRODUCTION

The *Memoirs* of James Touchet, Earl of Castlehaven, and *A Letter from a Person of Honour in the Countrey* by Arthur Annesley, Earl of Anglesey, represent the positions taken by two of the factions involved in the Irish civil war of the 1640s. The Confederate Catholic rebellion was one of the most significant events in Irish history, for as a result most Englishmen characterized all Irish Catholics as perfidious and barbarous. No longer was a distinction made between loyal and disloyal Catholics. Castlehaven's career reveals the dilemma faced by one of the major political and religious groups in Ireland, the Catholic royalists. According to his own account, Castlehaven opposed the Confederate Catholic rebels at the beginning of the insurrection in October 1641, but after the lords justices refused his assistance against the rebels and, on little evidence except his Catholicism, accused him of treason, he decided to take refuge with the Confederates. Castlehaven was a talented military leader and he rapidly became one of the most important generals on the Confederate side. Probably because he objected to the influence of those who refused to accept a peace with the royalists, he broke with the rebels during the summer of 1646 and joined the forces led by Lord Lieutenant Ormond, with whom he had family connections. Castlehaven was absent from Ireland when Ormond reached a temporary accommodation with the Long Parliament, but he returned with the Lord Lieutenant in 1648 and for the next three years fought for the royalist cause.

Arthur Annesley, who later became Earl of Anglesey, represented another faction, the Puritan "New English" who had gained wealth in the Ulster plantations of the early seventeenth century. His father, Baron Mountnorris, had run afoul of Viscount Wentworth, Charles I's Lord Deputy of Ireland in the 1630s, and had been condemned to death. Although the sentence was never executed, it is not surprising that Annesley supported the Long Parliament against the King. He was in Ireland in 1641, but in marked contrast to Castlehaven he seems to have fled to England rather than accept the troops offered him by the government to battle the rebels. In 1645, Annesley returned to Ireland as one of the Parliamentary governors of Ulster. He attempted to convince Monro's Scottish forces and Ormond's royalists to unite behind the leadership of Parliament to defeat the Confederates, whom he called "the vilest of people."[1] He was not immediately successful, but in 1647, when Ormond's position became desperate and he decided to accept Parliamentary control of Dublin, Annesley was one of the commissioners who received the royal insignia. During the next decade, the careers of Annesley and Castlehaven continued on different courses. After being expelled from Parliament in Pride's Purge and briefly retiring from politics, Annesley became reconciled to most aspects of the Cromwellian settlement and served in Richard Cromwell's 1659 Parliament as a member from Dublin. Castlehaven, on the other hand, went into exile on the continent. The political situation after 1660 may, however, have brought the two men more closely together on some issues. Castlehaven returned to Britain at the restoration of the monarchy and was rewarded for his loyalty with a pension. Annesley supported the Stuarts at the right moment and received an earldom and the lucrative office of Vice Treasurer of Ireland. He eventually rose to the position of Lord Privy Seal, and, until his vote for exclusion in 1680, he usually supported the King in the House of Lords. If his testimony can be credited, he and Castlehaven often voted together in Parliament.

The composition of both Castlehaven's *Memoirs* and Anglesey's *Letter from a Person of Honour* was related to Anglesey's plans to write "The General History of Ireland from the First Footsteps thereof in Antiquity to this Time." He had been gathering material for this book since the early 1660s but it was not until January 1680, that he began to concentrate on its composition. His manuscript, if he ever completed it, has been lost. Fortunately, Herbert Wood (in *Analecta Hibernica* 12) identified his notes for the history in the British Museum.[2] These notes indicate that his book would have been primarily a diatribe against the Irish Catholics, but it might have contained valuable documents which have since disappeared. Anglesey hoped to obtain copies of material which "I saw in one of the garrets over the rooms which are used for the [Irish] Privy Council's sittings" where they were treated "but as waste paper when I was there."[3]

Anglesey began his work by approaching others for evidence relating to the 1640s. Among those from whom he requested material were the dowager Countess of Orrery, Henry Jones the Protestant Bishop of Meath, Dr. Edmund Borlase the son of one of the lords justices of the early 1640s and the author of *The History of the Execrable Irish Rebellion,* and the Earl of Castlehaven. Castlehaven probably realized that Anglesey's history would not treat the Irish Catholics fairly, and rather than making notes for Anglesey's private use he decided to publish his *Memoirs* covering his career to 1651. The 1680 edition was imperfect, for the publisher issued it before Castlehaven had finally approved the text. Castlehaven stopped the sale of the *Memoirs* but not before a copy reached Dr. Borlase, who must have been incensed at Castlehaven's remarks about the lords justices. In August 1680, Borlase informed Anglesey of the publication of the *Memoirs* and begged his "censure thereon,"[4] and at the end of the month, Castlehaven himself sent Anglesey a copy of the book. Because he was responsible for the composition of reminiscences condemning the actions of some Irish Protestants, Anglesey felt it necessary to reply to Castlehaven's arguments. *A Letter from a Person of Honour* was at first meant to be read only by Castlehaven, but (probably at the end of October) his pamphlet was published anonymously. It was postdated "1681".

Anglesey admitted that he had written the *Letter,* but he denied in public and in private that he was responsible for its publication; "it got abroad," he complained in a letter to Borlase, "by the general liberty taken to print anything."[5] Whoever arranged for the publication of the *Letter* during the hysteria of the Popish Plot must have realized that it would arouse great controversy, for it not only drew attention to the "massacre" of Protestants by Catholics but it also implied that the Duke of Ormond, who was again Lord Lieutenant of Ireland, sympathized with Catholicism. Despite Anglesey's denials, Ormond believed that Anglesey had indeed authorized the printing of the *Letter.* The pamphlet was, Ormond feared, part of a Whig campaign to force his resignation or recall from Ireland. Shortly after the pamphlet appeared in print, Anglesey joined the Whigs in voting to exclude the Catholic Duke of York from the throne, and Ormond's friend, Sir Robert Southwell, reported that the Earl of Shaftesbury, the opposition leader, said, "it was a seasonable book and worth its weight in gold."[6] On the other hand, K. H. D. Haley in the most recent biography of Shaftesbury argues that the Whig leader did not support an attack on Ormond in 1680. Moreover, Anglesey's diary records no contact with the opposition during the period in which he wrote his *Letter*. In short, except for the timing of the *Letter's* publication and Southwell's unsubstantiated evidence, there is no sign that Anglesey was acting under Shaftesbury's influence. It would seem that Anglesey did not want his manuscript to be printed but rather to circulate privately among his acquaintances in order to excuse his role in the writing of Castlehaven's *Memoirs*. It is likely that the printer stole a copy of the manuscript and issued it anonymously so that Anglesey would not learn of its publication until it had had a profitable sale.

Ormond was furious at Anglesey's pamphlet and wrote several lengthy replies which were never published.[7] Rather than engage in a pamphlet war with Anglesey, however, Ormond brought his objections to the *Letter* to the English Privy Council in June 1682. Charles II, who was displeased at Anglesey's exclusion vote, used the opportunity to dismiss him from the office of Lord Privy Seal. The Privy Council decided that the booklet was a "scandalous libel" and at the same meeting also condemned Castlehaven's *Memoirs*.[8] Anglesey retired to his country estate at Blechington, Oxfordshire, to continue work on the history of Ireland. His surviving notes indicate that his hatred of the Irish Catholics had not diminished. Castlehaven enlarged his *Memoirs* to include his activities to 1678, and a new edition appeared in 1684, under the title, *The Earl of Castlehaven's Review.* (It is this version, containing Castlehaven's complete reminiscences, which is reproduced herein.) Despite the Privy Council's decision, neither man was willing to revise his opinions on the Irish civil war.

Historians have long recognized the importance of Castlehaven's *Memoirs* as a major source of data on the military engagements of the Irish rebellion. For the most part it is an accurate account of Castlehaven's activities, although in emphasizing the consistency of his royalism he may have misrepresented some of his motives. Anglesey's *Letter* is more polemical than historical. He included little information about his actions during the 1640s; probably, as a member of Charles II's government, he was not anxious to admit that he had represented the interests of the Long Parliament in Ireland. But the importance of these two works is not limited to their factual accuracy. In writing about many of the same events from the Catholic royalist and "New English" viewpoints, Castlehaven and Anglesey reflected the political and religious tensions in seventeenth-century Ireland.

DOUGLAS G. GREENE

Old Dominion University
Norfolk, Virginia

NOTES

1. Oxford. Bodleian Library. MS Carte 17, f. 465.
2. London. British Museum. Additional MS 4816.
3. Dublin. National Library of Ireland. MS 2481, pp. 13-14.
4. London. British Museum. Additional MS 22,548, f. 93.
5. Idem. Sloane MS 1008, f. 293.
6. Oxford. Bodleian Library. MS Carte 98, p. 65.
7. London. British Museum. Additional MSS 34,770 and 34,771.

8. For details see James Butler Ormonde, *A True Account of the Whole Proceedings Betwixt his Grace James Duke of Ormond, and the Right Honor. Arthur Earl of Anglesey Late Lord Privy-Seal, Before the King and Council, and the said Earls Letter of the Second of August to His Majesty on that Occasion. With a Letter of the now Lord Bishop of Winchester's to the said Earl, of the Means to Keep Out Popery* . . . (London: T. Fox, 1682). Cited here according to Library of Congress main entry, this work is mistakenly attributed to James Butler, Duke of Ormond. It is quite clearly anti-Ormond, and there is solid evidence that Anglesey compiled the documents included in it, and wrote the introduction and connecting material.

THE Earl of *Castlehaven*'s REVIEVV:

OR HIS MEMOIRS

OF HIS

Engagement and Carriage

IN THE

Irish Wars,

Enlarged and Corrected.

WITH AN

APPENDIX and POSTSCRIPT.

London, Printed for *Charles Brome* at the Gun in St. *Pauls* Church-yard. 1684.

THE Earl of *Castlehaven*'s REVIEW: OR HIS MEMOIRS

OF HIS Engagement and Carriage IN THE 𝔍𝔯𝔦𝔰𝔥 𝔚𝔞𝔯𝔰, Enlarged and Corrected.

OF all the Practices used of late to Involve the Nation in a General Combustion, and once more to set us all together by the Ears, as nothing is more unchristian, so none can be of more dangerous Consequence to the Publick, than the Peoples rubbing up old Sores, and Reproaching one another (when they promise to Reform, and become Peaceable Subjects) with their past Crimes, or with the Names of Parties and Factions, to keep the Breach still on Foot. It has always been so Destructive of the Peace and Quiet of all Common-wealths, that there can be no hopes of a Lasting Settlement, while this Animosity continues. Hence it was that immediately upon his Majesty's most happy Restoration, it was thought of absolute necessity by the Representative Wisdom of the Nation, by King, Lords, and Commons, to Pass an Act of Oblivion of all Crimes till then committed, and by certain Penalties to stop the Peoples mouths from using any words of Reproach tending to revive the memory of their past Calamities. But such is the Licentiousness of this Libelling Age, and so great is the Malice, and so prodigious the Impudence of some wicked men, whose Charity extends no further than their Interest; that while

while themselves are the greatest Criminals, they exclaim against others, as unworthy to live. Of this we have several Instances in divers Books and Pamphlets by them published these forty years past, and some with no good design reprinted since these last troublsom times. But they have exceeded all others, and outdone even themselves, in the Tragical Storys they give us of the *Irish* Insurrection in the Year 1641. Which they have so strangely misrepresented to the World, and with such Fictions and Invectives traduced the whole Nation, that wherever they are believed, an *Irish-man* can pass for no other than a Monster in Nature.

'Tis true, the *Irish* Insurrection can never be justified, and had they alone been concerned in such Crimes, it were very reasonable, and just, if Prudence as well as Charity did not oblige us to forget and forgive, to have them exposed to the World, and set forth in the blackest Colours. But when their Neighbour-Nations were

were at least equally Criminal; 'tis no more Equity in any man to raile against them in particular, than 'tis Prudence in a Magistrate to shut up only one House when the Plague is Universal.

I must aver, I little expected to have any occasion this time of the day to speak or write any thing on this Subject, when I hoped all was forgiven and happily buried in Oblivion. But finding my self mentioned afresh, not without some new Aggravations, by these worthy Authors of Slander and Lyes, as having had a part in the *Irish* Rebellion; (tho left they should do me some Justice, they are not pleased to tell how I have been used before I was brought to it, nor how I carried my self while of that Party, nor yet what I have since done to expiate my Offence, by serving with all possible Zeal and Fidelity the late and present King ever since the Peace there concluded in 46.) I find my self under a necessity to say something in my own Defence, by setting forth the

the truth of my story, in as brief and plain a method as possible, to obviate the false and Malicious Calumnies of these forging Scriblers. But before I go farther, I must desire the Reader to make some difference between the first beginners of the Rebellion, and those that afterwards carried on the War under the title of the Confederate Catholicks of *Ireland*. And to shew what ground there is for this Distinction, I shall here give a short account of the Rise and Progress of that Insurrection, and begin with my conceptions on the Motives and Inducements, the Lord *Macguyre*, Sir *Phelim Oneile*, and others their accomplices, had to enter into that wicked Conspiracy.

After the *Scots* had Rebelled against the King in the Year 1638. though they soon laid down their Arms on the pacification at *Barwick*, where I was, yet the fire was but smothered for that time, not altogether extinguished. For in the Year 1640. it broke out with greater violence, than

than before, when they Invaded *England*, fought and beat the King's Troops at *Newborn*, and advancing took *Newcastle*.

On this Alarm the King came to *York* where he Assembled his Great Council of all the Peers of the Kingdom, amongst whom I was one; and by their advice the Treaty at *Rippon* was set on foot, where a suspension of Arms was concluded with the *Scots*, on condition to pay them above 25000*l. per* Month, to the great Discredit of the *English Nation*. All this time the King was importuned with Petitions from most Counties of *England* for a speedy Parliament; to which his Majesty agree'd: and having Dissolved his Great Council of Peers, he ordered that unfortunate Parliament to be Summoned, which met at *Westminster*, the third of *November* following.

Great was the Peoples expectation concerning the Resolutions of this new Parliament; having in about 12 years before seen none, but that short one

one of *April* preceding, which lasting but two and twenty days, spent for the most part in idle Preliminaries and declamatory Harangues, came not to any issue touching the publick Affairs of the Nation. The King at the opening of this Session, sets forth how the *Scots*, without any Cause or Provocation, came in an horrible manner Arm'd into *England*, were then gnawing the Bowels of the Kingdom, and like so to continue, unless speedily prevented by his and their joynt Concurrence. In order therefore to reduce these Gentlemen, he gives both Houses all possible assurance of his readiness to concur with them in any thing they could find effectual for setling the Peace and Redressing the real Grievances of his Subjects. But this, and many other such Gracious Condescentions, served only to increase the Flame among the Factious, who now, instead of Voting the *Scotch* Army Rebels and Traitors, not only stiled them Dear Brethren, but bestowed on them 300000 *l.* for their kindneſs, and Voted Mr. *Gervaſe Holles* to be expel'd the Houſe, for ſaying, upon their debate how this Money ſhould be paid, *That the beſt way of paying them was by Arms to expel them out of the Kingdom.* Neither was this all. The *Scots* are no more careſſed on the one hand, than the Kings Miniſters and Friends are run down on the other: and the more the good King gave way to their madneſs, and yielded to their moſt unreaſonable demands, in hopes they would at laſt become Sober, and mind their Duty, the more Inſolent and Imperious ſtill they grew; as if nothing but the total Subverſion of the Government could in any meaſure ſatisfie their Ambition. Which though they carried ſmoothly for ſome time, till they had got themſelves firſt made *Triennial* and at laſt Perpetual Dictators, and by ſending the Biſhops to the Tower had Robbed their Prince of twenty ſix Votes at once, and of a great deal more by Paſſing the Bill of *Attainder*; yet

yet nothing was more visible in all their proceedings, than their ill Designs against the Monarchy, and thereupon the approach of a sudden Rupture between the King and the Factious part of both Houses.

 The Lord *Maguyre*, Sir *Phelim Oneile*, and others of the *Irish* Nation dissatisfied with their own Condition, and consequently weary of the Government there, thought this Conjuncture very seasonable for their purpose: and like the Asse in the Apologue (who by imitating the fawning Dog expected to get into his Masters favour, but was soundly bastinado'd for his folly) doubted not but by taking the like method, they should fare no worse than the *Scots* in the Redress of their Grievances. And therefore that they should not lose the advantage of so fair an Opportunity, they quickly put their heads together, and concluded that on the 23*d.* of *October* 1641, they should Surprize the Castle of *Dublin*, the chief Magazine of the Kingdom:
         and

and upon their good Succeſs in that Attempt, endeavour to take in the reſt. But Providence timely diſcovered this wicked Conſpiracy, and the Plotters fell into the Pit themſelves digged for others: *Macguire*, and *Mackmahon* were taken, and being ſent into *England*, Executed at *Tyburn*, and the reſt forced to retire into Woods and Mountains to ſave themſelves from the hands of Juſtice.

Now the *Iriſh* offered me, while I was among them ſeveral Reaſons (beſides theſe mentioned) why they would at this time enter into ſuch a horrid Combination againſt their Natural Soveraign. But theſe following, I think, are the moſt conſiderable.

Firſt, They obſerved, that by the Governors of that Kingdom they were generally looked upon as a Conquered Nation, ſeldom or never treated like Natural or Free-born Subjects: and for their farther excuſe ſaid beſides, that diſcontented people, while thus uſed, are very apt to think they are no longer obliged,
than

than they are forced, to Obedience; but may by the same way they had lost, when able, regain their Liberty.

Secondly, It grieved them extremely, that on the account of *Tyrone*'s Rebellion, as they said, six whole Counties in *Ulster* were in a lump escheated to the Crown, and little or nothing restored to the Natives, though several of them never joyn'd with *Tyrone*, but a great part bestowed by King *James* on his Countreymen.

Thirdly, It did not a little heighten their discontent, that in the Earl of *Strafford*'s time there was a great noise of intitling the Crown to the Counties of *Roscomon*, *Mayo*, *Galway*, and *Cork*, with some parts of *Tipperary*, *Limericke*, *Wicklow*, and others: and they averred that experience tells us, where the Peoples Property is like to be Invaded, neither Religion nor Loyalty is able to keep them within bounds, if they find themselves in a condition to make any considerable Opposition: and so brought in the saying of those resolute Ambassadors of of the *Privernates,* who tho reduced to such a very low condition, that they came to beg Peace of the Senate of *Rome,* yet being asked what Peace should the *Romans* expect from them that had broke it so often? they boldly answered, (which made the Senate accept of their Proposals) if a good one, it shall be faithful and lasting; but if bad, it shall not hold very long. For think not (said they) that any People, or even any man, will in that Condition, whereof they are weary, continue any longer than of necessity they must. *Liv. lib.* 8.

Fourthly, They found that since the Sitting of this Parliament great Severities were used against the Roman-Catholicks in *England,* and both Houses sollicited by several Petitions out of *Ireland* to have those of that Kingdom treated with the like Rigor. which to a People so fond of their Religion as the *Irish,* was no small inducement to make them, while there was an opportnnity offered, to stand upon their Guard.

Fifthly,

Fifthly, They saw the *Scots* by pretending Grievances, and taking up Arms to get them Redressed, had not only gained divers Priviledges and Immunites, but got 300000*l.* for their visit, besides 850*l.* a day for several Months together. And this Precedent encouraged the *Irish* so much at that time, that they offered it to *Owen OConally*, who discovered the Design, as their chief motive of Rising then in Rebellion. Which (said he) they engag'd in, to be rid of the Tyrannical Government that was over them, and to imitate *Scotland*, who by that course had enlarged their Priviledges. *OConally's* Exam. *Octob.* 22. 1641. *Borlases* History of the *Irish* Rebellion. p. 21.

Lastly, They foresaw the Storm draw on, and such misunderstandings daily arise between the King and Parliament, as portended no less than a sudden Rupture between them. which made these Male-contents believe, the King thus engaged, partly at home, and partly with the *Scots*, could

could not be able to suppress them so far off; and therefore rather than hold out, would grant them any thing they could in reason demand, at least more than otherwise they could expect.

Much to this purpose Mr. *Howel* writ of the original of this Rebellion in his *Mercurius Hibernicus* in the year 43. whose words, because an Impartial Author and a known Protestant, I will here transcribe in confirmation of what I have said, and for the Readers farther satisfaction. *The Irish hearing* (faith he) *how well their next Neighbours had sped by way of Arms, it filled them full of thoughts and apprehensions of Fear and Jealousy, that the* Scot (*than whom no Nation upon Earth is in that perfection and with greater Antipathy hated by the* Irish) *would prove more powerful hereby; and consequently more able to do them hurt, and to attempt ways to restrain them of that Connivance which they were allowed in point of Religion.— Moreover they entred into Consideration, on*, that they also had sundry Grievances and Grounds of Complaint, both touching their Estates and Consciences, which they pretended to be far greater than those of the Scots. For they fell to think that if the Scot was suffered to introduce a New Religion, it was reason they should not be punished in the Exercise of their Old, which they glory never to have altered. And for temporal matters, wherein the Scot had no Grievance at all to speak of, the new Plantations, which had been lately a foot, to be made in Connaught *and other places*; the concealed Lands and defective Titles, which were daily found out; the new Customs which were Imposed; and the incapacity they had to any Preferment or Office in Church and State, with other things, they conceived to be Grievances of a far greater nature, and that deserved Redress much more than any the Scot had. To this end they sent over Commissioners to attend this Parliament in England with certain Propositions; but they were dismissed hence with a short and unsavoury Answer,

Answer: which bred worse blood in the Nation than was formerly gathered. And this with that leading case of the Scot, may be said to be the first incitements that made them rise.

2. In the course of humane Actions we daily find a true Rule, *Exempla movent*, *Examples move and make a strong impression upon the Fancy*; Precepts are not so powerful as Precedents. The said Example of Scotland wrought so wonderfully upon the imagination of the Irish, and filled them (as I touched before) with thoughts of Emulation, that they deserved altogether to have as good usage as the Scot; their Countrey being far more beneficial, and consequently more importing the English Nation. But these were but confused imperfect Notions, which began to receive more vigour and form after the death of the Earl of Strafford, who kept them under so exact an Obedience, tho some Censured him to have screwed up the strings of the Harp too high, that the taking off of that Earls head, may be said to be the second incitement
to

to the head of that Insurrection to stir.

3. Add hereunto that the Irish understanding with what acrimony the Roman-Catholicks in England were proceeded against, since the Sitting of our Parliament, and what further designs were on foot against them, and not only against them, but for ranversing the Protestant Religion, which some shallow-brain'd Schismaticks, throw into the same Scales with Popery; they thought it was high time for them to forecast what should become of them, and how they should be handled in point of Conscience, when a new Deputy of the Parliaments Election, approbation at least, should come over. Therefore they fell to consult of some means of timely prevention. And this was another motive, and it was a shrewd one, which push'd on the Irish to take up Arms.

Lastly, That Army of 8000. men which the Earl of Strafford had raised to be transported into England for suppressing the Scot, being by the advice of our Parliament here Disbanded, the Country was annoyed by some of those stragling Soldiers, as not one in twenty of the Irish, will from the Sword to the Spade, or from the Pike to the Plow again. Therefore the two Marquesses that were Ambassadors here then from Spain, having propounded to have some numbers of those Disbanded Forces, for the Service of their Master; his Majesty by the mature advice of his Privy-Council, to occur the Mischiefs that might arise to his Kingdom of Ireland, by those loose Cashiered Soldiers, yielded to the Ambassadors motion, who sent notice thereof to Spain accordingly, and so provided Shipping for their Transport, and impressed Money to advance the business; But as they were in the height of that Work, his Majesty being then in Scotland, there was a sudden stop made of those promised Troops, who had depended long on the Spaniards Service, as the Spaniards had done on theirs. And this was the last, though not the least, fatal Cause of that horrid Insurrection. All which particulars

particulars well considered, it had been no hard matter to have been a Prophet, and standing upon the top of Holy-Head, *to have foreseen those black Clouds, Ingendring in the* Irish *Air, which broke out afterwards into such fearful Tempests of blood. Out of these premises it is easie for any common understanding, not transported with passion and private Interest, to draw this conclusion: That they who complyed with the* Scot *in his Insurrection; they who dismissed the* Irish *Commissioners with such a short unpolitick Answer; They who took off the Earl of* Strafford's *Head, and afterwards delayed the Dispatching of the Earl of* Leicester; *They who hindred those Disbanded Troops in* Ireland *to go for* Spain, *may be justly said to have been the true causes of the late Insurrection of the* Irish.

Thus concludes this Learned and Ingenious Gentleman, who, as being then his Majesties *Historiographer*, was as likely as any man to know the transactions of those times, and as an *English-man* and a Loyal Proteſtant, was beyond all Exception of Partiality or Favour of the Papiſts of *Ireland*; and therefore could have no other reaſon, but the love of Truth and Juſtice, to give this Account of the *Iriſh* Rebellion, or make the *Scotch*, and their wicked Brethren in the Parliament of *England*, the main occaſion of that horrid Inſurrection. Neither was this the ſingle Opinion of Mr. *Howel*, but the common ſentiment of all honeſt and knowing Men, confirmed even by the dying words of our Royal Martyr in the twelfth Chapter of his *Eikon Baſilike*, where he ſaith, *Certainly it is thought by many wiſe men, that the prepoſterous rigor and unreaſonable Severity, which ſome men carried before them in* England, *was not the leaſt incentive that kindled and blew up into thoſe horrid Flames, the ſparks of Diſcontent which wanted not pre diſpoſed fuel for Rebellion in* Ireland; *where deſpair being added to their former diſcontents, and the fears of utter*

utter Extirpation *to their wonted Oppressions, it was easie to provoke to an open Rebellion a People prone enough to break out to all exorbitant Violence, both by some Principles of their Religion, and the natural desires of Liberty; both to exempt themselves from their present restraint, and to prevent those after rigors, wherewith they saw themselves apparently threatned by the covetous zeal, and uncharitable fury of some men, who think it a great Argument of the truth of their Religion, to endure no other but their own. And again: I believe, it will at last appear, that they who first began to embroil my other Kingdoms, are in great part Guilty, if not of the first letting out, yet of the not timely stopping those horrid Effusions of blood in Ireland.*

'Tis plain therefore, tho other motives were not wanting to render many of that Nation ill affected to the Government and prepare them for Violence, the unexpected success of the *Scots* and the daily misunderstandings between the King and the Parliament in *England*, gave at this time birth and life to the *Irish* Rebellion. For I must confess, I am my self now, as I have been long since upon serious Reflections abundantly convinced, that however the circumstances of *this time gave life and birth* to that Rebellion of *Ireland*; yet the design of it had been laid partly at home, but chiefly abroad in Foreign Parts, even several years before the troubles either of *England* or *Scotland* began. And that the original, true and great motive indeed thereof was no other than that *fatal one* which for so many hundred years from *Hen.* II. to the beginning of King *James*'s Reign had been not only the very source of all the dangerous Rebellions of that Country; but the very bane and ruine of its People on all sides for so many ages. The National Feud, I mean, betwixt the *meer Irish* (as the *ancient Milesians*

sians are called) and *later Irish*, or Colonies of *English* extraction among them: and the unalterable perswasion of the former, that the *English Conquest* of that Country was but meer Usurpation without any just Title: and that the right both to the Supream Sovereignty and Proprietorship too of all the Lands of *Ireland* still remained according to the ancient *Brehon* Laws of that Country (which say they, had never been Legally Repealed or Antiquated) and consequently also according to the Laws of God) in the Surviving Heirs of the more ancient Natives, the *Milesians*. It is true that forty years continual and flourishing Peace in all obedience to the *English* Laws there, from the last of Queen *Elizabeth* to 1641. seemed to carry a fair outside, as if all those National former Animosities and pretences had been utterly extinguished. But alas! the old leven still fermented inwardly of one side: and among that side the fire was but cover'd under hot Embers.

Embers. The Earls of *Tirone* and *Tirconel*, and the Councils of *Spain* and *Rome*, and the *Irish* Monasteries and Seminaries in so many Countrys of *Europe*, and very many of the Churchmen returning home out of them, and chiefly the titular Bishops, together with the Superiors of Regular Orders, took an effectual course, under the specious colour of Religion, to add continually new fuel to the burning coals, and prepare 'em for a flame on the first opportunity; which whoever did not see in the beginning of this Rebellion, (as many did not) by observing what extraction or what names all the first Appearers in it were of: and how particularly of the whole hundred that were designed for seizing the Castle of *Dublin*, there was not so much as one person of *British* blood, extraction, or name among them: might nevertheless, and without the help of any multiplying glass, most clearly see it in the procedure of the War. Certainly in my opinion, 1. That whole and great and
most

moſt numerous Party's exclaiming every where, both at home, in *Ireland*, and abroad in other Countrys, againſt the *very firſt Ceſſation* concluded with the Kings Lieutenant the Marqueſs of *Ormond*: and in foreign Courts repreſenting thoſe Confederates that concluded it, not only as falſly aſſuming the name of *Iriſh* men, but as really favouring the Schiſm and Hereſies of *England*. 2. Their forcing after, at the end of three years more, both the Repreſentatives and whole Body of the *Iriſh Confederates* to reject ſo ſcandalouſly and perfidiouſly as they did the Peace of 46. 3. Their oppoſing ſo long, and in ſuch manner as they had done the *Peace* of 48. till it was too late to retrieve it, or ſubmit to it: were ſuch arguments, as upon ſerious reflection might convince any unbyaſſed perſon, what the primary grand deſign and Original ſourſe of that Rebellion was; and what alſo the natural end of it muſt have been, if ſucceſs had anſwered the expectation of the

the great contrivers, in their Plot for seizing the chief Magazine of the Kingdom, the Castle of *Dublin*.

And yet I must withal acknowledg, there has been from the very beginning of the Rebellion a considerable number of those very ancient *Milesians*, that upon all occasions sided still with such other Confederate Catholicks as endeavoured all they could to bring back the whole Nation to their former Obedience to the King and his Laws. In that number the Lord Viscount *Muskry* (after Earl of *Clancarty*) with his whole Party the *OCallaghans* and some other Gentlemen thereof men of note in *Mounster*, were eminent. To whom, after the Nuncio's Excommunication published against those that obeyed the Cessation of Arms concluded with the Lord of *Inchiquin*, many others also of the said *Milesians* in other Provinces joyned themselves in order to the Peace of 48. and consequently their return to the King. Among these, besides the Lord of *Iveagh*, *Alexander mac Donel*, and others, even that unfortunate gentleman Sr. *Phelim ONeill* himself was one, tho after all, I must likewise acknowledg that because the far greater number of the *Milesians*, at least stronger Party of them was on the other side, their wilfull Obstinacy rendred at long run all the endeavors and returns of honest men wholly unsignificant and fruitless whether to the King or themselves, or to defend their Country from being utterly subdued at the end of three years more by the Parliament Forces.

But if any peradventure think otherwise either of the different inclinations and endeavors of those Partys among the *more ancient Irish* themselves, or of that very Original design and sourse of the Rebellion which I have nakedly given according to my own later thoughts of both: yet forasmuch as I put here no stress at all on such matters, I pass them over: and only at present aver, That whatever the primary grand Design, whatever the sourse of this Rebellion was, or
might

might have been; it is notwithstanding in all appearance beyond dispute, that (as I have said before) the unexpected Success of the *Scots*, and the daily misunderstandings between the King and the Parliament in *England*, was that which gave it *Birth and Life at this time, viz.* on the 23. of *October* 1641. As for the Massacre that ensued, it was certainly very barbarous and inhumane, though I cannot believe the tenth part of the *Brittish* Natives (reported by Sir *John Temple* and others of the same kidney to have been murdered by the *Irish*) lived then in that Kingdom out of Cities, and walled Towns, where no such Massacre was Committed. I am certain in Sir *John Temple*'s Muster-Rolls, of whom the subsequent Scriblers borrowed all their Catalogues, there are not 50000 persons to be found, though 'tis manifest that in divers places he repeats the same people and with the same circumstances twice or thrice over, and mentions hundreds, as then murdered, that lived

ved many years after, Nay, some even this day alive. Nevertheless, 'tis very certain, that there have been great cruelties committed upon the *English*, tho I believe not the twentieth part of what is generally reported. But the truth is, they were very bloody on both sides, and tho some will throw all upon the *Irish*, yet 'tis well known who they were that used to give Orders to their Parties sent into the Enemies Quarters, to spare neither Man, Woman, nor Child. And the leading men among the *Irish* have this to say for themselves, that they were all along so far from favouring any of the Murderers, that not only by their Agents soon after the Kings Restoration, but even in their Remonstrance presented by the Lord Viscount *Gormanstown* and Sir *Robert Talbot* on the 17th of *March* 1642. the Nobility and Gentry of the Nation desired, That the Murders on both sides committed should be strictly examined

See *Borlase* his *History* p. 58.

amined, and the Authors of them punished according to the utmost severity of the Law. Which proposal certainly their Adversaries could never have rejected, but that they were conscious to themselves of being deeper in the Mire, than they would have the World believe.

This is plain matter of Fact, and the consequence of it so obvious, that notwithstanding all the groundless Clamors of some, who loudly cry out against the *Irish*, but speak not a word of their own Rebellion, I must do that Kingdom so much Justice, as to declare that I can no more believe the leading part of the Nation did ever design, much less encourage, the Barbarous Cruelties there committed, than I can be perswaded that the Lords and Commons, who first made War against the late King in *England*, did from the beginning intend to imbrue their hands in his Sacred blood. Yet still I think them inexcusable, because I see no great difference, whether a man kills another

ther himself, or unchains a fierce Mastiff, that will tear him to pieces. I cannot therefore but believe the Contrivers of the *Irish* Rebellion and their Abettors guilty of the Massacre that ensued, tho committed by the rude Rabble, no less than those that raised the late Rebellion in *England*, as guilty of their Princes blood, as if they had actually been Regicides; tho the Army on the one hand, and the Rabble on the other, did the work, which their first movers, who unchained them from their Obedience to the Laws, were not able to hinder.

As for the generality of the Nation, whatever the *Northern* Rebels gave out to the contrary, to encourage their Party, and induce others to joyn with them: 'tis manifest, they knew nothing of the Design before, nor favoured it after it was discovered; as appears by their solemn protestation in Parliament on *November* 16. 1641. when meeting according to their Prorogation in the
Castle

Castle of *Dublin,* and this Rebelliion being laid before them by the Lords Justices, Sir *William Parsons* and Sir *John Borlase,* in order (as they said) to find out some effectual means to reduce the Rebels, and bring them to Justice, both Houses immediately declared their abhorrence to the Rebellion, and agreed *Nemine Contradicente* to the following Protestation.

'Whereas the happy and peacea-
'ble state of this Realm hath been of
'late and is still interrupted by sun-
'dry persons ill-affected to the Peace
'and Tranquillity thereof; who con-
'trary to their Duty and Loyalty to
'his Majesty and against the Laws of
'God and the fundamental Laws of
'this Realm, have Traiterously and
'Rebelliously Raised Arms, Seized
'upon his Majesties Forts and Castles,
'and Dispossessed many of his Faith-
'ful Subjects of their Houses, Lands,
'and Goods, and have slain many of
'them, and committed other Cruel
'and Inhumane Outrages and Acts of
'Hostility within this Realm: the
'said

'said Lords and Commons in Parlia-
'ment Assembled, being justly mo-
'ved with a right Sense of the said
'Disloyal and Rebellious Proceedings
'and Actions of the Persons afore-
'said, do hereby Protest and Declare
'that the said Lords and Commons
'from their hearts do Detest and Ab-
'hor the said Abominable Actions,
'and that they shall and will to
'their utmost power, maintain the
'right of his Majesties Crown and
'Government of this Realm, and the
'Peace and safety thereof, as well a-
'gainst the Persons aforesaid, their
'Abettors, and Adherents, as also a-
'gainst all Foreign Princes, Poten-
'tates and other Persons and attempts
'whatsoever; And in case the per-
'sons do not repent of their aforesaid
'Actions, and lay down Arms, and
'become humble Suitors to his Maje-
'sty for Grace and Mercy, in such
'convenient time, and in such manner,
'and form as by his Majesty or the
'chief Governor or Governors and
'the Council of this Realm, shall
'be

'be set down; The Lords and Com-
'mons do further Protest and Declare,
'that they will take up Arms, and
'will with their Lives and Fortunes
'suppress them and their Attempts,
'in such a way, as by the Authority
'of the Parliament of this Kingdom
'with the Approbation of his most
'excellent Majesty, or his Majesties
'Chief Governor, or Governors of
'this Kingdom, shall be thought most
'effectual. See *Burlase's* Hist. p. 33.

Thus both Houses of Parliament, the true Representative of the Nations Loyalty unanimously declared their readiness to Prosecute and Suppress the Rebels, and in order to bring them speedily to condign Punishment; having with all possible Zeal and Alacrity, offered their Lives and Fortunes to the Lords Justices, they fell immediately to consider of the most effectual means to do the Work. But this way of Proceeding did not it seems, square, with the Lords Justices Designs, who were often heard to say, that the more were in Rebellion, the

more

more Lands should be forfeit to them; and therefore in the very heat of the business they resolved upon a Prorogation: Which the Parliament understanding, the Lord Vicount *Castelloe* and my self, were sent from the Lords House and others from the Commons, to the Lords Justices, to desire the continuance of the Parliament at least till the Rebels (then few in number) were reduced. But our Address was slighted, and the Parliament the next day Prorogued, to the great surprize of both Houses, and the general dislike of all honest and knowing men.

This encouraged the Rebels, and vastly increased their numbers in divers places of the Kingdom. Freedom of Rapine and Murder, drew such numbers of men together, that the few desperate Malecontents, who began the Tragedy, in a short time became a formidable Army, and were at length so bold, as to Besiege *Drogheda*, about twenty miles from *Dublin*: to the Succour of which Major *Roper* Marching with 7 or 800 men, was in a great mist (near *Gillianstown*) set upon by the Rebels and defeated; whereupon they forced the Country round about, (as the *Scots* the year before did the Northern parts of *England*) to a Weekly Contribution, for the Payment of their Army, which afterwards was by the Lords Justices made a great Crime, (though in the North of *England* the like was thought none by the King) as if the Contribution favoured and encouraged the Rebellion.

The Members of Parliament in this Disorder retired to their several Habitations in the Country; so did I to mine, but had not been long at home, when I receiv'd a Letter Signed by the Viscounts of *Gormanstown*, and *Nettervile*, and by the Barons of *Slane*, *Lowth*, and *Dunsany*, with an inclosed to the Lords Justices, which these Noble-men desired me to send, and if possible, to get their Lordships Answer. the Letter was very humble and submissive, desiring only they might have permission to send their

Petiti-

Petitions into *England*, to represent their Grievances to the King: wherefore I sent it inclosed to the Lords Justices, who were silent as to theirs, yet answered mine, tho little more than a Covert; in which they said, these Lords were Rebels and Traitors, and advised me to receive no more Letters from them. I readily submitted, nor do I know to this hour, how that Letter came to my hands.

All this while Parties were sent out by the Lords Justices, and Council from *Dublin*, and most Garisons throughout the Kingdom, to kill and destroy the Rebels; but the Officers and Soldiers took little or no care to distinguish between Rebels, and Subjects, but killed in many places promiscuously Men, Women, and Children; which procedure, not only exasperated rhe Rebels, and induced them to commit the like Cruelties upon the *English*, but frightned the Nobility and Gentry round about, who seeing the harmless Country People, without respect to Age, or Sex, thus barba-

barbarously murdered, and themselves openly threatned as favourers of the Rebellion, for paying the Contribution they could not possibly refuse, they resolved to stand upon their Guard. Nevertheless, before they would attempt any thing against the Government, they sought several ways to get their Petitions conveyed to the King, and at length prevailed with Sir *John Read* a Scotch-man, and one of his Majesties Servants, (then going for *England*) to undertake it; who coming to the Marquess of *Ormond* upon his March towards *Drogheda* was (on what Suspicion I know not) by him sent to the Lords Justices to *Dublin*, and not concealing what he carried, by them Imprisoned, and soon after put to the Rack. Much about this time was the like done to *Patrick Barnwell* of *Kilbrew*, a man of 66 years of Age, but upon what account I cannot tell; only have been told, his Crime was that he came in upon the Lords Justices Proclamation of Pardon to those

those of the Pale, that would in ten days submit themselves; and was so wise, as not to consider that Free-holders (as being more Criminal *Borlase p. 30.* than the rest, because of their Estates) were by the Lords Justices expresly excepted out of that Proclamation. As to *Read*, several questions were put to him, and among the rest, he was much pressed to tell, how far the late King, and Queen were privy to, or concerned in the *Irish* Rebellion: this is notoriously known; but I have it more particularly from my brother Coll. *Mervin Touchett*, who heard it from Sir *John Read* himself, as he was brought out of the Room, where he was Racked.

This did not a little enflame the reckoning, and it was a great addition to their discontent, that the King referred the whole business of *Ireland* (whereby they thought he deserted the protection of his People) to the Parliament of *England*, who thereupon passed such

C 4 wild

wild Votes and Ordinances, as tended to the utter extirpation of the Natives of that Kingdom; not only declaring on *December* 8. 1641. that they would never give consent to any Toleration of the Popish Religion in *Ireland*, or in any other his Majesties Dominions, *Burlase*, p. 34. but enacting further in *February* following, when few of any considerable fortune, or Estate were concerned in the Rebellion, that two Millions and five hundred Thousand Acres of profitable Land in *Ireland*, besides Bogs, Woods, and Barren Mountains, should be assigned to adventurers for small proportions of money (which was afterwards employ'd to raise Armies against the King in *England*) to reduce the Rebels of that Kingdom. But the greatest discontent of all, was about the Lords Justices proroguing the Parliament, the only way the Nation had to express their Loyalty and prevent their being misrepresented to their Sovereign; which had it been permitted to sit for any

any reasonable time, would in all likelihood without any great charge or trouble, have brought the Rebels to Justice. For the War that afterwards ensued, was headed and carried on principally by Members that sate then in Parliament. And to say these members were all along concerned in the Rebellion or engaged with the first contrivers of it, is to make them not only the greatest knaves, but the veriest fools on Earth, since otherwise they could not have been so earnest for the continuance of the Parliam. whilst sitting in the Castle, and under the Lords Justices Guards, who upon the least Intelligence, which could not long be wanting, had no more to do but to shut the Gates, and make them all Prisoners, without any possibility of escape or hopes of Redemption.

Thus the Contagion spread it self by degrees over the whole Kingdom, and now there's no more looking back, for all were in Arms, and full of Indignation;

tion; Fighting there was almost in every corner, and very unfortunately for me; one encounter hapned in the sight of my House at *Maddingstown*, between the Marquess of *Ormond* Commanding the *English*, and the Lord Viscount *Mount garrett* the *Irish* Forces, where the latter was defeated. This Encounter goes by the name of the Battel of *Killrush*, fought the 15th of *April*, 1642. The *English* were not above 3000 men strong, but were bold and expert Troops well Officer'd, with some Commons; the *Irish* were more in number, but ill Armed, and but newly formed into Bodies.

After this defeat my Lord of *Ormond* being to pass with his Army, just by my Gates, some of his Officers of my acquaintance, came Galloping before, assuring me his Lordship would be with me in half an hour. Hereupon I bestirred my self, and having two or three Cooks, a good Barns door, and plenty of Wines, (for besides my own Family,

I had with me the Dutchess of *Buckingham*, the Marquess of *Antrim*, her Husband, and the Lady *Rosse*, Mr *Daniel*, his Sister) we patched up a Dinner ready to be set upon the Table at my Lord's coming in; But some that came with him turn'd this another way, magnifying the entertainment beyond what it was, and published through the Army, that it was a mighty Feast prepared for my Lord *Mount-garrett*, and the Rebels. This through the *English* Army passed for currant, and I believe did me no small prejudice, with the Lords Justices, as shall appear by the sequel of my story, which I shall now pursue with a Letter I received from my Brother, Coll. *Mervin Touchett* upon this Occasion.

Hearing your Lordship is now writing somewhat again of your concerns in Ireland *during the late War: tho I, as one that was with you there in the beginning of the Troubles, and therefore possibly might mind you of some Passages*

ges more in my knowledge than yours, have before written to you on that subject; yet now remembring some things I had then omitted, I add them here.

When the Rebellion broke forth in the North, *you were in* Mounster: *and on the News, you immediately repaired to* Dublin, *to the Lords Justices, Sir* William Parsons, *and Sir* John Burlace, *where you acquainted them with your willingness to serve the King against the Rebels, as your Ancestors had formerly done in* Ireland, *on like occasions: to which they reply'd, your Religion was an Obstacle. There being then a Parliament in that Kingdom Sitting, you were resolved to see the event, sending me to your House at* Madingstown, *in the County of* Kildare, *to secure and defend it, in case there were any Rising in those Parts. Upon my coming, I found many poor* English *stript, whom I took into the House and Relieved, defending them in the best manner I could. Some time after, the Parliament being Dissolved, you desired of the Justices a Pass to go for* England.

gland. *But they refusing, you acquainted them that your Estate there was not in a condition to maintain you in* Dublin; *and desired that you might be supplied with some mony, for your subsistance, until such time that you could apply your self to the Parliament in* England *for a Pass to bring you over; which they denied. You prest them then to direct you what course you should steer. To which they replyed:* Go home and make fair Weather. *You took this Advice, and being come, my Lord of* Antrim *and my Lady Dutchess of* Buckingham, *soon followed; and you were very well pleased with so good company to spend your Provisions. But in a short time, the* Irish *came and drove away a great part of your flock to a Village near. It being night, you desired me to take your Servants and endeavor the recovery; which I did, bringing with me two or three of the chiefest Conductors of this Rabble. This enrag'd the* Irish *so much, as you conceived I was not safe there: and therefore sent me to* Dublin, *to attend the Justices Orders,*

and

and assure them of your readiness to return on a call, they *sending a Convoy. Which they promised to do, as occasion required. When I went from you, you thought it necessary that I should take with me, all the poor* English *that were saved; and to let them go with the Carts, which were loaden with Wool for* Dublin; *leaving only one of them, who was a Sadler, then my Lord of* Antrim's *Servant. In the Passage near* Rath-Cool, *the Rebels fell upon them, and barbarously killed some, and wounded others: my self and one more escaping by the goodness of our Horses. But a Servant of mine governing the Carts, and being an* English *man they took: And whilst they were preparing to hang him, Sir* John Dungan's *Eldest Son,* Walter Dungan, *came forth of his Fathers House with a Party, and rescued him with the rest of those that were left alive, and brought them safe to* Dublin, *where I was gotten.*

In a few days after, the Marquess of Ormond *sent out a Party towards the place where this murder had been committed.*

mitted, *I went with them, and coming near, we met Sir* Arthur Loffeus *Governor of the* Naſſe *with a Party of Horſe and Dragoons, having killed ſuch of the* Iriſh *as they met.*

But the moſt conſiderable Slaughter was in a great ſtrength of Furſe, ſeated on a Hill, where the People of ſeveral Villages (taking the Alarm) had ſheltered themſelves. Now Sir Arthur *having inveſted the Hill, ſet the Furſe on fire on all ſides, where the People being a conſiderable number, were all burnt or killed, Men, Women and Children. I ſaw the Bodies and the Furſe ſtill burning.*

The Sadler that I had left in my Lord of Antrim's *Service ſome time after met me, complaining, that coming for* Dublin *he had been taken by the Rebels by means of a Boy that Served your Lordſhip, and if I would not give him forty Shillings, being he was damnified, (in ſo much) he would complain. I told him, that the Boy he mentioned was no Servant of yours; but kept out of Charity, and to whip the Dogs out of doors:*
being

being blind of an Eye, and lame of a Leg. He reply'd, that altho he were blind and lame, he had a Note from my Lord of Antrim to have him apprehended by those that were neither blind nor lame, which he gave to them, who took him Prisoner, and carried him to the Garison of Leixlipp, kept by the Rebels. I bad him do what he pleased: for I would not give him one Farthing.

The next I heard of it, was, that he had complained; and that your Lordship was Indicted of High Treason. Upon which I made my addresses to the Lords Justices again, to let them know, tha they had not kept their Words with me, in suffering this Clandestine Proceeding against my Brother; but however, I would go and fetch you; and to that purpose desired them to let me have a Party of Horse. But that they refused. I then came down to you with some of my friends, and acquainted you with what had past. You answered, that you knew nothing of it, and went immediately with me to Dublin; where you addressed your self to my Lord of Ormond,

Ormond, *as I did my self in your behalf to the Lords Justices and Council, to acquaint them that you were come. They reply'd, that they could say nothing to it, till you appeared before them. Which you did the next day; and then they Ordered you to come the day following. At which time without calling you in, they committed you to Mr.* Woodcocks *House, one of the Sheriffs of* Dublin. *Now I seeing this rigorous usage towards you, with such bloody doings on all sides, and having been refused a Pass for my self to go for* England, *made a shift to get away in a small Boat, and go directly to the King at* York, *and Petition him that you might be sent for over to be Tryed here by your Peers. But his Majesties Answer was, that he had left all the Affairs of* Ireland *to the Parliament. Upon which I went to* London, *and Petitioned the Parliament to the same effect. Their answer was, that they could do nothing without the King; of which I gave you an account by Letter. This was the last Correspondence I had with you, being*

D *after*

after that continually serving his Majesty in England. *But the King coming from* Newark *to* Oxford, *he sent me with Dispatches to my Lord Leieutenant, and ordered me to go to you, and use my endeavours to perswade you to hasten a Peace. You received the Commission as very agreeable, saying, that from the beginning of the War you had always laboured for a Peace, and that you hoped it would soon be done. Before I returned, I saw it Proclaimed: and it goes by the name of the Peace of Forty Six.*

London, *July* 6. 1683.

Thus you have seen by my Brother's Letter, how, and upon what account I was made a Prisoner, by the Lords Justices, and no hopes left me of any relief from either King or Parliament of *England*; But was after twenty weeks Imprisonment, ordered to be removed from the Sheriff's House to the Castle: This startled

led me a little, and brought into my thoughts the Proceedings againſt the Earl of *Strafford*, who confiding in his own Innocence, was voted out of his Life, by an unprefidented Bill of *Attainder*. Befides, I heard nothing almoſt whilſt I was in Prifon but rejoycings at the Kings Misfortunes, and the ill fuccefs of his Arms then engaged in actual War with his Rebellious Subjects in *England*. The Lords Juſtices, and moſt of the Council, were too plainly of the Parliament Faction, and the Marquefs of *Ormond*, whom I knew moſt faithful to the King, fell defperately fick of a Fever, not without fome fufpicion of Poifon, and was then given over by his Phyficians. Hereupon I weighed well my own Circumſtances, and concluding that Innocence was a fcurvy Plea in an angry time, I refolved to attempt an Efcape, and fave my felf in the *Iriſh* Quarters; which I effected in this manner.

After the Battel of *Kilbruſh*, there was one *George Ledwidge*, an *Iriſh* Trooper of the Marqueſs of *Ormond*'s Army left wounded at my Houſe; who being recovered (in acknowledgment of kindneſs received) often viſited me in Priſon. I found ſo much fidelity in the man towards me, that I truſted him with my Deſign, and deſired his aſſiſtance. The Trooper overjoyed to hear I had that confidence in him, declared he was ready to venture his own life to ſave mine, and would value no danger to free me from that reſtraint. With this, immediately I gave him money to buy me three Horſes, for my ſelf, and two Servants with Saddles and Piſtols, and ordered him to have them ready at a certain place, againſt next morning This he punctually performed, and the night following, juſt as the maid was to ſhut the door, it being ſomewhat dark, I ſlipt into the Street, leaving my two men in the Houſe, and appointing them where they

ſhould

should find me in the morning. About nine of the Clock they came out of the House, and bid the maid make no noise, pretending I was not well, and had not rested that night. They no sooner came to me, The Guards of the Town withdrawn, and the Patrolles come in, but I sent them before with the Troopers son to get our Horses ready; the Trooper and my self soon following; but I, as his man carrying a Saddle under my Arm. To be short, we mounted all on Horseback, Marched as Troopers, carelesly out of Town, and took our way by *Temple-oag*, through the Mountains of *Wicklow*, towards *Kilkenny*. But before Dinner my escape was discovered by the People of the House, and on notice given to the Lords Justices, I was pursued by a Party of Horse, taking their way to my House, at *Maddingstown*. In the night they invested it, but not finding me (after they possessed themselves of what they could find) they killed many of my Servants and burnt

burnt my House; This I saw as I passed by, and had notice by the way, that *Castle-haven* also was seized by the *English*, and all I had there pillaged, and destroyed.

On my arrival at *Kilkenny*, I found the Town very full, and many of my Acquaintance, all preparing for War. To this end they had chosen amongst themselves, out of the most eminent Persons, a Council, to which they gave the Title of the Supreme Council of the Confederate Catholicks of *Ireland*, and formed an Oath of *Association*, by which all were bound to obey them. They had made four Generals for the Respective Provinces of the Kingdom; *Preston* of *Leinster*, *Barry* of *Munster*, *Owen Roe O'Neale* of *Ulster*, and one *Burke* of *Connaught*; and being to give Commissions, they caused a Seal to be made, which they called the Seal of the Council.

I was sent for to this Council, to tell my story, where I gave them a particular account of my Adventures;

tures; and being asked what I intended to do, I anſwered, to get into *France*, and from thence into *England*. Hereupon they told me their Condition, and what they were doing for their preſervation, and natural defence, ſeeing no diſtinction made, or ſafety, but in Arms; perſwading me to ſtay with them, being I was beloved in the Country, had three Siſters married amongſt them, was perſecuted on the ſame ſcore they were, and ruined ſo, that we had no more to loſe, but our lives. I took two or three days to think of this Propoſition, and to examine the *Model of Government* they had prepared againſt the meeting of the General Aſſembly, and moſt particularly their Oath of *Aſſociation* which was as followeth,

The Oath of Association.

I A, B. *Do Profess, Swear, and Protest before God, and his Saints, and his Angels, that I will, during my life, bear true Faith and Allegiance to my Sovereign Lord* Charles *by the Grace of God, King of Great* Britain, France, *and* Ireland, *and to his Heirs and Lawful Successors: and that I will to my Power, during my Life, defend, uphold, and maintain, all his and their just Prerogatives, Estates and Rights, the Power and Priviledge of the Parliament of this Realm, the Fundamental Laws of* Ireland, *the free exercise of the* Roman-Catholick *Faith, and Religion, throughout this Land, and the Lives, just Liberties, Possessions, Estates, and Rights of all those that have taken, or shall take this Oath, and perform the Contents thereof: and that I will Obey and Ratifie, all the Orders and Decrees made, and to be made, by the Supream Council, of the Confederate*

rate Catholicks *of this Kingdom, concerning the said Publick Cause:* and
*that I will not seek directly or indirect-
ly, any Pardon or Protection, for any
Act done, or to be done touching this
General Cause, without the Consent of
the* Major *part of the said Council:
and that I will not directly or indirectly
do any Act or Acts; that shall prejudice
the said Cause; but will to the hazard
of my Life, and Estate, Assist, Prosecute, and Maintain the same.*

*Moreover I do farther Swear, that
I will not accept of, or submit unto, any
Peace, made or to be made, with the
said* Confederate Catholicks, *without
the Consent and Approbation of the* General Assembly *of the said* Confederate Catholicks. *And, for the preservation and strengthening of the Association, and Union of the Kingdom,
that upon any Peace, or accommodation
to be made, or concluded with the said*
Confederate Catholicks, *as aforesaid,
I will, to the utmost of my Power insist
upon and maintain, the ensuing Propositions, until a Peace as aforesaid be made,
and*

and the matters to be agreed upon in the Articles of Peace, be Established and secured by Parliament.

So help me God, and his Holy Gospel.

Having spent some time on these thoughts, and at last taken my resolution, I returned to the Supreme Council, thanked them for their good Opinion of me, and engaged my self to run a Fortune with them. Whether Anger and Revenge, did not incline me to it, as much as any thing else, I cannot certainly resolve. This I well remember, that I considered how I had been used, and seen my House burning as I passed by; besides, that I was a light man, with no Charge, and without any hopes of redress from the King, who was then ingaged in an Intestine War. Now being thus a Confederate, and having taken the Oath of *Association*, they made me one of the Council, and General of the Horse, under *Preston*. The

The first Assembly met the 24th of of *October*, 1542. It differed little from a Parliament, but that the Lords and Commons sate together. They approved without delay all the Council had done, and setled a *Model of Government*, viz, That at the end of every General Assembly, the *Supreme Council* should be confirmed or changed, as they thought fit. That it should consist of twentyfive, six out of each Province, three of the six still resident, the 25th was my self, with no relation to any Province, but to the Kingdom in General. Every Province had a Provincial Assembly, which met on occasions: and each County had Commissioners for Applotting Money within themselves, as it came to their shares, on the General Applotment of the Province. Many other things there were as to Government, but these are the most remarkable.

The General Assembly being ended, the Supreme Council sent Envoys to the King of *France*, Mr. *Rotchford*, and

and after him, Mr. *Geoffery Barron*: To the King of *Spain*, F. *James Talbott*, an *Augustine Fryar*: To the Pope, First Mr. *Richard Belling*, after him the Bishop of *Ferns*, and Mr. *Nicholas Plunkett*. Besides these they had Residents with all these Princes, but they were generally Churchmen. The King of *France* first sent them in return Mr. *La Monarie*, to whom succeeded Mr. *Du Moulin*, and after him M. *Talloon*. The King of *Spain* first sent M. *Fuysott* a *Burgundian*, to whom succeeded the Count of *Beerhaven*, after him *Don Diego de'los Torres*. The Pope sent one *Starampo* Priest of the *Oratorian* Order, who remained till the coming of *Rinuccini* Arch-Bishop and Prince of *Fermo*, in quality of Nuncio. All this while the Generals were not idle, & mine took in *Burras*, *Fertfaulkland*, and *Byrrh*, in the Kings County; where I was with him, and had the good fortune to begin my Command in the Army, with an Act of Charity; for going to see this Garrison of *Byrrh*, before it Marched out,

out, I came into a great Room, where I found many People of Quality both men and women.

They no sooner saw me, but with Tears in their Eyes they fell on their Knees, desiring me to save their Lives. I was astonished at their posture, and petition, and having made them rise, asked what the matter was? they answered, that from the first day of the War, there had been continual action and bloodshed between them and their *Irish* Neighbours, and little Quarter on either side; and therefore understanding, that I was an *English* man, begged I would take them into my Protection. I knew there was two much reason for their Fears, considering they were to March two or three days through the woods of *Iregan,* and wast Countrys, before they came to *Athy,* their next Friend Garrison. I went therefore to the General immediately, and got to be Commander of their Convoy, and to make sure I called out 300. Foot, and 200. Horse, in whom

I had most Confidence, and carried off the people, who were at the least 800. Men, Women and Children, and though sometimes attaqued I delivered them with their Baggage safe to their Friends. Our next undertaking was on the 5th of *October*, 1642. Col. *Muncke*, since made Duke of *Albermarle*, having relieved *Ballniekill* a Castle in the Queens Country, General *Preston* overtook him near *Timachoo* in his retreat, and pressed him so, that he was forced to fight. In number they were pretty equal, about 1500 Horse and Foot each, without Cannon: but the business was soon over, and not many killed before we were routed: and had the Enemy pursued, it being a plain Country, and no Garrison near, we had certainly lost most of our Foot. This Check made us pretty quiet till towards the Spring following; then the Marquess of *Ormond* Lieut. General of the *English*, Marched from *Dublin*, in the Head of 3000 Horse and Foot, and some Cannon, and coming through the

the County of *Wexford* Besieged *Ross*, a considerable Town seated on the River *Barrow*. To relieve this Place, General *Preston* hastned with an Army of 5 or 6000 Horse and Foot, but no Cannon; and having sent 1500 Men Commanded by Leiut. General *Purcell*, into the Town, he Marched himself to *Temple-Wodigan* about two Miles from *Ross*, the Principal Pass by which the Marq. of *Ormond* must retreat, if he raised his Siege; as he did soon after the Succour got in; and finding *Preston* before him in Battle, knew not well what to do, being in an Enemies Country, and scant of Provisions. The Pass was at least half a mile through a Bogg, where no more than four Horse could march in a Breast, with water in some places up to the Belly. But *Preston* had not the Patience to expect the Enemies coming to him, which they must do or starve, but went over this Pass to them, and put himself under as great disadvantage as his Enemy could wish. The Marquess of *Or-mond*

mond took hold of this unexpected advantage, and gave *Preston* no time to form his Army into Battel, but Charged still as they went over, besides what he did all along with his Cannon; till at length after a considerable loss of men, killed and taken Prisoners, we were wholly routed and defeated. This goes by the name of the Battel of *Ross* fought, *March*, 18. 1642.

The Marquess being returned to *Dublin*, Jealousies and discontents broke out between him and some great ones there, which gave *Preston* leisure to raise another Army, and Besiege the aforesaid *Ballynekill*; where having Intelligence that Col. *Crawford* was Besieging *Ballybrittas*, a Castle belonging to the Viscount *Clamnaleer.* He sent me with a Party of 1500 Horse and Foot to relieve the Place; whereupon *Crawford* drawing off, in the Passing the River *Barrow* had his thigh broken in a Skirmish with a Musket shot. I returned as *Ballynekill* was Surrendred, and

and conveyed that Garrison too, as I had done the other at *Birrh,* safe to their Friends.

After this I remained at *Kilkenny* with the Supream Council, and *Preston* with his Army went into *Westmeath*: of whose absence the Enemies Garrisons in the County of *Catharloe* and *Queens* County taking advantage, they Alarm'd the County of *Kilkenny* to the very Gates of the City. To oppose these, I was commanded by the Council to gather what Forces I could, to Succour and secure the Country. I quickly got together about 2000 men, with some pieces of Cannon; and though the Enemy retired, yet I Marched on to *Ballenunry* in the County of *Catharloe,* and took both that and *Clahgrenan*; where the County of *Wexford* Regiment mutinied, but were soon reduced, and some examples made, serve well for the future. I marched thence to the *Queens* County, and Besieged *Ballihenan* Commanded by the *Grimes'es* a valiant People with a strong Garrison.

son. But a great Breach being made, when we expected they would Surrender, word was brought us there was a strong Party coming by the way of *Athy* to relieve them. I was not well at the time of this Alarm, but lay upon my Bed in my Tent; yet I made no great matter of it, knowing the Succour could not be considerable. But the Viscount *Mountgarret* being abroad, he sent me word they were coming on in great haste, and stronger than I thought, both in Horse and Foot, and were then near the end of the *Tougher*; which was a great way cut through a Bog, and I believe about half a Mile in length. Now I had a strong Guard of Horse and Foot at my end of the *Tougher* with a Line thrown up before them; so that I judged the danger was not great; however, I got on horse-back with 400 Horse, and as I came to my Guards, seeing some of the Enemy on the *Tougher* in their March towards us, I commanded them to follow me to meet the Enemy, thinking to have fought

fought them upon the *Tougher*; but they seeing us advanced, retired, and (while I was passing the *Tougher*) formed on a Plain two Musquet shot off; but when they perceived I was preparing to Charge, they drew off again, and did not stand me till they had got through a Gap in a Ditch with Water up to the belly; which having passed, they lined the Ditch with Musquetteers, drawing up their Horse and Foot close by to defend the Gap. Sir *Walter Butler* with his Squadron begun the Fight; but he being wounded in the Ditch with a Pike through his Thigh, his men fell off, and a second Squadron Charged, and did the like. But the Enemy seeing more Squadrons coming on, they took their advantage in the Smoak to run away, which we could not see till the Smoak was over. Then we followed but could not engage them till they recovered *Athy*, which was not far off. I guessed them to have been about 300 Horse and about 7 or 800 Foot. Their Succour

being thus beaten in their view, the Besieged Garrison yielded on condition to march out with their Arms. While this Place was putting in Order I went with a Party of Horse to *Baleadams* a Castle about a Mile distant belonging to Sir *John Bowen* Provost-Marshal, an old Soldier, and my long acquaintance. I sent to speak with him, and after some kind expressions, told him, I must put a Garrison into his Castle. He flatly denied me, and calling for his wife and two very fair daughters he had, desired only one favour, that in case I was resolved to use violence, I would shew him where I intended to plant my Guns, and make my Breach. I satisfied his Curiosity, and asked him what he meant by this question? because (saith he) swearing with some warmth, I will cover that part or any other your Lordship shoots at, by hanging out both my Daughters in Chairs. 'Tis true the place was not of much Importance, however this Conceit saved it. All this while my
Ld.

Ld. *Inchiquin* was Master of the Field in *Munster*, having won some Battels, beaten the *Irish* in all parts, and in a manner subdued the whole Province to four or five Towns; and with these two he was now going to work, beginning with *Killmalocke* in the County of *Limerick*, having set down before it with an Army of 7000 men. This Alarm'd the General Assembly then sitting at *Killkenny*, but most particularly those of that Province, who after many Consults among themselves, concluded at last, to ask succour of the General Assembly, though they saw but little hopes of any in that Exigency, for *Preston* was far off with the Army. Wherefore opening themselves more clearly than perhaps they would have otherwise done, they laid claim to me, as having my Earldom and Estate in their Province, though I was an Officer of *Leinster*: Alledging further, that their General was old and unfortunate, and that if I had the Command all would joyn in the

defence

defence of their Country, and take new Courage. I was present at this Proposition, and though I had Ambition and Vanity enough, yet having no prospect of Success I thanked them for their good Opinion of me, but heartily opposed their motion. But my Lord *Muskry* since made Earl of *Clancarty* (my great friend and of that Province) desired the Assembly to command me by virtue of the Oath of Association. This they did, and ordered that my Commission (under the Seal of the Confederates to Command in Chief for that Expedition) should be immediately dispatched. I submitted, and being asked what Troops were near at hand, I answered, I knew of none, but of my own Life-Guard of Horse, 'tis true, I had observed many stragling Horse in Town, but they would not be brought together without Money. Some money was then given out, and by ten of the Clock the next morning I had engaged about eighty Horse, and put them under the Command of *Garret Talbott*, Brother to
Sir

Sir *Robert Talbott*: These with my Life-Guard Commanded by Captain *Fitzgerald*, commonly called *Garret Garrough*, made in all 120 Horse, and with them I marched, accompanied with my L. *Muskry* and some others of the Province, to the Frontiers of *Munster*, where I met about 120. Horse more, most Gentlemen, and formed into a Squadron. But at *Cashel* I was received by the General of the Province *Barry*, the Lieut. General *Purcell*, and some other Officers with 700 Foot. That night I had intelligence, that the Lord of *Inchiquin* had raised his Siege, and Marched with 4 or 5000 men into the County of *Kerry*, but had sent Sir *Charles Vavasor* with 16 or 1700 Horse and Foot to take in *Clohlea*, a Castle then belonging to the *Condons*; I marched immediately towards him, and before night Encamped within three Miles of him, a Mountain only between us. My Brother *Richard Butler* of *Kilcash*, Brother to the now Duke of *Ormond*, was sent out the same night to discover the Enemy, and in the Morning

ning word was brought us, that the Castle was taken, the Garrison after Quarter given put to the Sword, and my Brother Engaged. On this, I lost no time, but Marched in all haste with my Horse to his Succour: which joyned with his made but 240. or 250. at the most. The Foot Marched after, but the old General moved so slowly, that I had defeated the Enemy before he came within two Miles of the Place. The manner thus:

Sir *Charles Vavasor*, though he had taken the Castle, remained still in his Camp, till seeing me on the top of the Mountain above him, come to succour mine that were Skirmishing, he drew to Arms; but being amongst Hedges and Ditches, and the Castle between us, I could not come at him, till he Marched towards *Castle-Lyons*; where in a large Plain he drew up his Men: but I going by the advantage of a great Valley, came into the Plain unseen, almost as soon as he; and having ordered three or four Squadrons of Boys on Horse-back to possess the Ground from whence I came,

came, I lost no time in the Charge and quickly defeated his Horse, who to save themselves, broke in on the Foot and put them into disorder; Their Cannons were useless being past the Black-water. This with God's blessing and a great shower of Rain gave me the Victory, with little or no loss. Sir *Charles*, that Commanded, with several other Officers, remained Prisoners; their Cannon and Baggage taken, all their Foot defeated; but their Horse for the most part escaped. This hapned on a Sunday, the fourth of *June*, 1643.

Now having left the best advice I could for the improving this advantage, I took leave of the General, with others of the Province, and returning to *Kilkenny* gave the Assembly an account of what had passed, in order to their further Commands.

Soon after, the Assembly being broke up, and a Supreme Council Chosen to Govern in their absence, I return'd to *Kilcae* (my Brother *Butler*'s House) to rest my self. The Council went to *Ross*; and whilst they

they were there, a Trumpet brought them a Letter from the Marquefs of *Ormond,* fetting forth his being appointed by the King to hear our Grievances, and to treat for an accommodation. The Trumpet was quickly difpatched, with fome flight Anfwer; which coming to my knowledge, I repaired to *Kilkenny,* whither the Council was returned; and on information finding what I had heard was true, I fent for Sr. *Robert Talbott,* Sr. *Richard Barnwell,* Col. *Walter Bagnall,* and fuch others as were in the Town well affected, and leading men in the Affembly, though not of the Council, and having acquainted them with what I underftood, I told them if they would ftick to me, I would endeavour to give it a turn. We all agreed on the way, which was to go to the Council then fitting, to take notice of the Kings Offer, and their Return, and to mind them, that the Confideration and Refolutions concerning Peace and War, the General Affembly Referved served wholly to themselves; and therefore to require that they would send immediately a Trumpet of their own, with a Letter to the Marquess of *Ormond*, giving him to understand they had issued Summons for a General Assembly, in order to acknowledge the Kings gracious favour in naming him his Commissioner to hear and redress our Grievances. This we put in execution and gained our point without much Resistance.

The Marquess of *Ormond* being thus brought into a Treaty, the Confederate Commissioners met at *Siginstown* near the *Nasse*, as his Excellency had appointed, in order to a Cessation of Arms. At which time all Parties laboured to get what they could into their Possession. Col. *Moncke*, after made Duke of *Albemarle*, Marched into the County of *Wicklow* to take in the Harvest, and possess some Castles there. I was Commanded by the Council to make head against him, and having Rendezvouzed my Troops, consisting of about

about 3000 Horse and Foot, at *Ballinekill* in the County of *Catharloe*, notice was brought me, that Collonel *Moncke* was marched away in all haft to the Affiftance of the L. *Moore*, then facing *Owen, Roe, ONeale* near *Portlefter*. Finding therefore now I had nothing to do, I thought it worth my while to indeavour the taking in *Dollarftown, Tully, Lacagh,* and other Caftles in the County of *Kildare* between the Rivers of *Barrow* and *Liffee*. I began with *Dollarftown*, a Place about a Mile from *Kilcae*, where I had a Garrifon, and Marched from my Camp with three or four hundred Horfe, and about 300 Foot, and coming before the Place in the Evening, (for it was no more than fix or seven Miles) I fent a Trumpet to the Mafter of the Caftle Mr. *Dade*, who had been long of my Acquaintance. The Gentleman immediately came to me upon Summons, and I gave him Reafons why he fhould put the place into my hands.

He

He consented. But as the men, appointed to Garrison the Place, were Marching towards it, one Lieutenant *Burres* who came but that Afternoon from *Athy*, debauched the Soldiers within, and perswaded them to shut the Gates, and bid me defiance. This I saw was no fault of the Gentleman, whom I kept with me that night, and lodged at *Kilcae*; but immediately dispatched an Express to *Kilkenny*, for three good Battering Pieces. Next morning I returned to my Camp at *Ballynekill*, and the day following my Guns being come as far as *Catharloe*, I sent in the Evening a Party of Horse and Foot with Orders before day to Invest the Place. The morning following I arrived my self with the rest of my Forces and the Cannon, and without Summoning began to Batter: and having made a Breach, Stormed the Place, and set fire to the Gates; but the Gentlemans Wife and some others were suffered first to come out. The rest, (especially Mr. *Burres* and his Comrades)

rades) suffered as they deserved.

Having Mastered this Place, in the Evening I dispatched a Party of Horse and Foot to Invest *Tullygh*, which they did before day. In the morning I arrived my self, and having Planted my Guns Summoned the Place, and had it yielded by Sir *George Wentworth* then Governor, on Condition that both Horse and Foot might March out with their Baggage.

Having thus taken this Castle, and left a Garrison to secure it, I Encamped on a Heath called the *Currogh* of *Kildare*, from whence I Summoned all the Castles thereabouts and had them yielded; only whilst I was thus Encamped Coll. *Chidley Coote* Governor of *Lacach* came to me, and tho he had nothing to secure his return, yet on Conditions I let him go, but after appearing before his Place had it according to our Agreement.

This done, I repass'd the *Barrow* at *Minster-Even*, Marched into *Leix*, and took three or four small Places. But

But as I was going on, I had advice from the Commissioners at *Siginstown* that they had on the fifteenth of *September* 1643. concluded a Cessation of Arms with the Marquess of *Ormond*; to which I submitted.

After this a Treaty went on for a *Peace*, and in a short time all was agreed, except a Concession for Churches and the Splendid Exercise of Religion, as in *France* or *Spain*. This was much insisted upon by the Confederate Commissioners, and as resolutely refused by my Lord of *Ormond*, who alledged that the King (by agreeing to such an Article) might endanger the loss of his whole Party in *England*; and in truth it would have signified little to the Confederates; for their Security chiefly consisted in keeping up the King, and having Force enough in their own hands, which would have been sufficiently left them, tho twenty thousand of their men had been sent into *England*, along with the ten thousand men my Lord of *Ormond*

mond sent out of *Leinster* and *Munster* of the *English* Troops in those Provinces.

For at this time as all agreed to the Cessation, except the *Scots* in *Ulster*, so they would have submitted to any Peace, that should have been concluded between my Lord of *Ormond* and the Confederates; and thus united, the *Scots* and the rest of the Parliament Party there would have been soon forced to a Submission. It was certainly a great Folly; and a prodigious instance of blind zeal in the *Irish* Clergy to stand thus out with the King, after such repeated professions of Loyalty, and so many Battels lost by their Generals in the four Provinces of the Kingdom, who had not all this time won one single Victory from the beginning of the Confederacy, nor any Colour of success, but what little advantages I gained, as you have already seen.

Besides, it was very visible that the *Confederate Irish* could subsist no longer than the War lasted between the

the King and Parliament; and if upon any terms the King and they agreed, whether he forced them to a Submiffion, or was forced to comply with their infolent demands, as there was no poffiblity for the *Irifh* then to hold out, fo they could not in reafon expect any mercy from either, but Major General *Monroe* fome time before arrived in *Ulfter* from *Scotland* with ten thoufand *new Scots*, to whom Sir. *Robert Steward* joyned with five or fix Thoufand of the *old Scots*, Natives of that Province; and alfo fome *Englifh* under the Command of Sir *Awdley Mervin*, Sir *Theophilus Jones*, and others, would not fubmit to this Ceffation, but forced General *ONeale* to fo great Streights (who had been but a little time before Defeated by that Party in the encounter where *Con ONeale* and many others were killed) that in the beginning of Winter, leaving his Troops and *Crejaghts* to fhift the beft they could for themfelves, he came to the General Affembly sembly held at *Waterford*; where he set forth the lamentable condition of his People, desiring the assistance of the other three Provinces, and in the name of his own Province undertaking to joyn to their Forces four thousand Foot and 400 Horse; but withal declaring, that otherwise he with his Forces and *Crejaghts* should be obliged to save themselves in the other Peovinces; this last point of *Owen ONeal*'s Speech, (besides their perswasion that the *Scots* would not fail soon to follow and visit them, made the Assembly come to a quick conclusion, and agree to send six thousand Foot and six hundred Horse out of the other three Provinces. But it coming to the question, who should be the General of this Army, they went to the Election after this manner; the Assembly sitting, those they thought fit to come in competition, they caused their names one under another to be written down, and from each, a long line to be drawn; then at the Table

Table where the Clerk fate, every Member of the *General Assembly*, one after another, with a pen puts a dash on the line of him that he would have to be General; and to the end that none should mark more than once, four or five were chosen out of the Assembly, (two of which were Bishops) being upon their Oath, to overlook this marking. Now contrary to *Owen ONeal's* expectation who had designed this Generalship for himself, by which he would be *Generalissimo*, I hapned to be chosen, which *Owen Roe* took extremely to heart, as I have reason to believe. However he carried it fairly, and came to congratulate and wish me good Success; giving withal great assurances of his performance, and readiness to serve me to the utmost of his power. Next day a Commission was sent me with Orders to prepare all things for this Expedition; which I did, and made some enquiry into the matter. But the farther I looked into it, the worse I liked it; for I considered

sidered I was now to make a War not only in a Country where I had never been, but where we had not so much as one City or Walled Town, and the Enemy had many.

That by all intelligence, I found the *Scots* could draw into the Field sixteen or seventeen thousand men. That if *Owen ONeale* should perform and deal fairly with me, yet all I was to expect, did not exceed ten thousand Foot and one thousand Horse. That having no Towns in *Ulster*, we should be forced to bring all our Provisions from the other Provinces where I had my Magazines. That I must depend upon *ONeale* for Intelligence, for by such Lights I always guided my self in my former small undertakings. But that which most of all troubled me, was, that I did not see how I could avoid a Battel if the Enemy had a mind to it; being I was to make an offensive War. I had also this other consideration to discourage me, that altho our Parties had commonly the better, yet our Armies

Armies had alwaies the worſt. This was experimented in ſeveral Battels and Rencounters; and the reaſon thereof was clear and obvious. For moſt of all the great Towns in the Kingdom were the Enemies, and Garriſoned, and of the few we had there was none but *Killkenny* would receive a Gariſon. So that at our leaving the Field in Winter, as the Enemy returned into their Gariſons; where they were with their Officers kept in Diſcipline, ours were diſperſed all over th Kingdom into little Villages and odd Houſes, never ſeeing an Officer till the next Campaigne. And therefore came to their Rendezvouz in the beginning of every Field, like new men half chang'd. And for the Horſe they were ſo haggled out in riding up and down to ſee their Friends, that they ſeemed hardly able to draw their legs after them; and both Horſe and Foot with ruſty Arms not fixed: But how plainly ſoever I ſaw my ill condition, I muſt through as well as I could; yet withal resolving to avoid a Battel with all possible means, and seek to make my War by Parties and Surprizes. Now having time enough before the Campaigne, I was commanded by the Supreme Council to march into *Connaught*, to reduce some of our own Party, which had set up for themselves in the County of *Mayo*, and were possessed of *Castle-Carrow* and *Castle-Barr*, the former Commanded by one *Bourke*, the latter by the Lord *Mayo*. I took with me two thousand men, passed the *Shanon* at *Fort-Faulkland*, and by the Marquess of *Clanrickards* permission, marched through his Country. These Castles made little resistance, and being yielded I sent my Party under the Command of Sir *James Dillon* into the County of *Roscomon*, to reduce the *Ormesbyes* and some others, that held Garisons there, and would not submit to the Cessation. When he had done his work (which he had quickly dispatched) he returned into *Leinster*, and lodged the Troops as he was

was ordered. But I went my felf ftreight to *Killkenny* to put all in order for the next Campaigne; yet ftill with fome miftruft of *Owen ONeale*'s performance. Wherefore I defired and prevailed with the Council to grant me four hundred Horfe and Dragoons more, in cafe I could raife them, as I did, without Charge to the Country.

The firft Rendezvouz I made in order to this Field, was about Midfummer, 1644. at *Granard* in the County of *Longford*; where I had appointed three thoufand Horfe and Foot, with two or three Field Pieces, to meet me; intending there to have expected the coming up of the whole Army; which might be in four or five days time; for *ONeale* was near Encamped at *Port-lefter*, and the reft Marching as Ordered. My Spyes, that met me at this Rendezvouz, and came in haft, all agreed they had left the Enemy near a certain Mountain threefcore miles off; that they were feventeen thoufand ftrong with one

F 4 and

and twenty days Provision, no Cannon nor other Baggage, and were ready to March. I thought my self pretty secure for that night; but before day one from *Cavan* (which was but twelve miles distance) assured me he had left the whole Army of the Enemy there, and that their Horse and Dragoons would be with me in the morning. On this advice I packed off as fast as I could, and gained *Port-lester,* having Ordered the rest of the Army to come thither; and at the Instant commanded a Col. with five or six hundred Foot and one hundred Horse to defend the Bridge of *Fienagh,* that I might not be pursued. It was of Stone, and a Castle on our end. I sent with him Shovels, Pickaxes and Spades, with plenty of Amunition. The Enemy according to my intelligence came at Sun-rising into the Camp I had left, and shewed themselves the next day before that Bridge: but my unfortunate Colonel sent over his Horse to Skirmish; and when they were far enough

enough out, on a sudden the Enemy mingled with them, which was the cause our Foot could do nothing, but through fear to kill their own, left Bridge, Castle, and all free for the Enemy. However it availed them little, for finding me well Posted, tho *ONeale* was of another opinion, their Provisions shrunk, and being at least twelve days march from their own Country, they stayed not to give me further trouble, but hastened homewards.

I was now at leisure to call on General *ONeale* for his 4000. Foot and 400. Horse, being resolved to follow the Enemy and try my fortune in *Ulster* as I was designed. He excused himself, by reason of the continual Alarms in his Country, that he could not at present make good his word; yet assured me, that so soon as I came into the Province, I should have no reason to complain. On this assurance, I marched on with my six thousand Foot, and one thousand Horse and Dragoons; and *ONeale* joyned

joyned with me about two hundred Horse, and three or four hundred Foot; his *Crejaghts* marching with us, and drew me on as far as *Toineragaoh*; where having intelligence that the Enemy had revictualled themselves, and were returning, to encounter me, I pressed *ONeale* very hard to make good his word; but he plainly told me he could not do it, alledging that his People were all amongst the *Crejaghts*, and every one looking to save what he had. In this sad condition, I blam'd my own weakness, that I was perswaded with fair promises to come so far into an Enemies Country, and with such a handful of men, to oppose a powerful Army; However I was resolved to see the Enemy, then encamped at *Dromore-Iveagh*; and therefore taking such Guides as *ONeale* would give me, and leaving the Command of the Camp to him, in the Evening I marched with my thousand Horse, and Dragoons, and fifteen hundred Foot towards *Dromore*. These I left on

on a Pass about three miles from my Camp, to make good my retreat, intending to fall with my Horse into their Horse-Quarter. But whether wittingly or willingly in my Guides, it was Sun-rising when I came within two miles of their Horse-Quarters. Nevertheless, tho I lost my Design, yet still I was resolved to see my Enemy. And to this end, perceiving some of their Horse at Grass, I drew up my men under a Hill, near a little River, where there was a stone Bridge, and sent a Party to take those Horses; which they did, and brought them to me. But the Enemies Guard of Horse being near, after my Horse were come back seized the Bridge and defended it. I sent men to beat them off; but it would not do; then I sent another Party; the same still: during this dispute, I perceived a Party of Foot coming over a great Plain; then I galloped down my self, with some Officers, and more Horse, and forcing the Bridge, I had the cutting of that Party of Foot, and took their
Com-

Commander, Captain *Blare* Prisoner: Whilst this was doing a party of mine pursued the Horse that ran from the Bridge; but before they overtook them, they were met with another, which routed them, and others of mine put them also to run. In short, before this Bickering ended, most of the Horse on both sides were engaged; the Enemy at last drew off and so did I to my Army. Being returned to my Camp, I acquainted *ONeale* with what had past: and how the Enemies Army were advancing, according to my intelligence. Whereupon he advised me to retire to *Charlemont*, a Fort where he had a Garison. I followed his advice, and found it a very good Post, there being a very large plain joyned to it, on the one side runs the *Black-Water*, and near the Fort a Bridge over it, the rest surrounded with Boggs and Moorish Grounds. My Horse lay Encamped at *Benboarb*, on the other side of the River. At the same time that I came into this place, *Manroe*, with his Army my arrived at *Ardmagh*, about two or three miles diſtant, and there encamped and fortified himſelf. Thus neither of us being able to engage the other, we lay in a pretty good Correſpondence, and the ſmall War we had was chiefly in cutting Parties and Convoys. During this idle time I went often to ſee my Horſe-Quarters, and being one day merry with the Officers, ſeveral Soldiers came about us, and in a pleaſant way I asked them what they would give to come to a days work with the Enemy? they anſwered, they would be glad of it if their doublets and skins could be made proof againſt the Launces of the *Scots*, of which they had many Squadrons. Having found this apprehenſion, I paſſed off the diſcourſe, and that night diſpatched an Expreſs to *Wexford*, where I had a Magazine, to bring me thence ſo many defenſive Arms as might cover two Ranks of my Horſe; which being come, and every day finding more difficulties I reſolved to march away;

for

for my Provision came much harder to me than the Enemies did to them; and *ONeale* began to be very weary of sometimes assisting me with Cowes; so that after two Months I resolved the endeavouring to gain my own Country, seeing no hopes of any Forces from *ONeale*. Which to effect (for I did not desire fighting) I caused a *Tougher* or great way to be cut through the Bogg near the Fort, leading to *Toineragaoh*, by which the Enemies Provisions came. Having finished this way, and knowing their days, I took time to pass over most of my Horse and some Foot, shewing them beyond the *Tougher* as if that night I intended streight for *Toineragaoh*, passed over the Bridge with the whole Army, leaving my Cannon and Baggage in the Fort with a strong Garison, plenty of Ammunition, and all the Provision I could possibly scrape to put in. That night I marched, and all the next day, taking a great Round before I could have my own County

on

on my back, which having obtained in the County of *Cavan*, I faced towards the Enemy, about five or six miles from them; which *Monroe* understanding, and finding I lay easier for my Provisions than he did for his, raised his Camp, and Marched home. It being now late in the year, and *Monroe* retired, I sent a Party of Horse and Foot to bring off my Cannon and what I left in the Fort of *Charlemont*, and so marched to *Fineagh*; where I met Commissioners from the *Supreme Council* to receive the Army, and lodge them on the three Provinces, together with fifteen hundred *Ulster* Men, who on my orders came to me out of *Connaught*, being of no Army, but endeavouring to live by strong hand, which I could not admit. Thus ended the *Ulster* Expedition, like to be so fatal to the *Confederate Catholicks of Ireland* thro the failing or something else of General *Owen Roe ONeale*. But after all, the three Provinces had no reason to complain of this Campaigne, for this

Army

Army they sent kept them from being troubled either with *Scots* or *Ulster* People that year.

Having thus left the Army with Commissioners, on Muster above eight thousand strong, (for I had been recruited with several Companies) I took my way to *Kilkenny*, ill pleased that the *Treaty* of *Peace* trained so long; and designed not to stir from the Council till I saw it concluded. But coming there, I found the *Supreme Council* in great consternation; for the Lord *Desmond* Governor of *Duncannon*, which commanded the Harbor of *Waterford*, was Declared for the Parliament; as also my Lord *Inchiquin* in *Munster*, who before had not only submitted to the Cessation, but sent a considerable number of his Troops, and himself followed soon after into *England* to serve the King, where having some disgust, as 'tis said, because the Residency of *Munster* was given to the Earl of *Portland*, he returns and declares for the Parliament, commanding

ing by their Commission as President of *Munster*. These of *Waterford* especially pressed the taking of *Duncannon*, making great offers to the Council of large Assistance: *Preston* is named for this work, it being within his Province, and is sent thither with three or four thousand Men, Miners, and a good train of Artillery. I had the curiosity to see this Siege, and will relate the particulars, because the only in form I saw in *Ireland*. He made no line of Circumvallation, fearing no Succour that could come on the land-side; but began his approaches with two Attacks, and being come near the place joyned them with a Line of Communication; and then ran them on, divided, to the Ditch before the Rampier; for it had no Counterscarpe or Bastions, but was fortified in reddant. Those within made a good defence and lost nothing in six weeks, only the Besiegers had made a Lodging on the edge of the Ditch. At this time two or three Parliament Frigats arrived

rived with succour of men, Ammunition and Provisions, and came to Anchor within less than Cannon-shot of the Fort. But before they could Man out their Boats, so terrible a Storm arose, that in eight or ten days none could come ashore. Whereupon those within being in despair, and pressed with want, were forced to yield.

All this while my Lord *Inchiquin* overran *Munster*, and coming to *Cashell* the People retired to the Rock where the Cathedral Church stands, and thought to defend it. But 'twas carried by Storm, and the Soldiers gave no Quarter; so that within and without the Church, there was a great Massacre, and amongst others more than twenty Priests and Religious men killed. Towards the Spring the *Supream Council* ordered me to go against *Inchiquin*, and to begin the Field as early as I could. The Enemy in this Province had always been victorious, beating the Confederates in every Encounter, having never

never received any Check but in that I mentioned at *Cloghleagh*: So that every Gentlemans House or Castle was Garisoned, and kept the Country in awe. To begin therefore this Field, I made my first Rendezvouz at *Clonmell*, and the Army Encamped not far from it. Thither came *Dean Boyle*, now *Lord Chancellor of Ireland*, and then married to my Lord *Inchiquin*'s Sister, his business was to perswade me to spare *Doneraile*, and other Houses and Castles not tenable. I answered, that I desired it as much as he, tho hitherto they had annoyed the Country, equally, as if they had been strong. I told him in short, I had orders to take all I could, and such as I thought not fit to Garison, to Destroy; yet if he pleased to cause the Garisons to be drawn out, and by Letters from the owners to put them into my hands; I would appoint some few men unto them with Commanders, in whom I most confided, and would make it my business to intercede to the Council to preserve them.

G 2   The

The *Dean* and I parted good friends. But whether he could prevail or no, with my Lord *Inchiquin* or the Owners, I know not; but I heard no more from him.

Soon after, that is about the fifth of *April* 1645. I marched towards *Caperquin*, my Army confifting of about 5000 Foot, and 1000 Horfe, with fome Cannons; and having viewed the place, I foon perceived where they miftook, that befieged it the year before, and after much time fpent with great lofs of men, were forced to quit it: There being a Town and a Caftle that commanded it, they attackt the Town, and I the contrary, the Caftle; which yielded; the Town could not refift; *Dromane* fell likewife into my hands. Whilft I was ordering thefe places, a Trumpet came to me, from the Lord *Broghill*, fince made Earl of *Orrery*, to let me know that he was on the great *Coney-warren* near *Lifmore*, where he fhould be glad to fee me. The Trumpet preffed my anfwer, swer, but I kept him with me, and immediately marched towards my Lord; but upon my coming near he drew off, and marched away.

From thence I wrote a Letter to the Commander of *Lismore*, a house of my Lord of *Cork's*, I think one *Major Poor*. I endeavoured to perswade him to put that place into my hands, and gave him many reasons, why I desired its preservation, as if it were my own. But he answered that his Honour was above all; that he would hold it to the last, and doubted not of timely Succour; so I left Major *Poor*, and Marched to *Michaelstowne*, which after some shot of Cannon was surrendred. Then having intelligence that 6 or 700 Horses were come over the *Black-water*, marching towards me, and at that time drawn up on a Hill in the great plain of *Roches* Country; I marched with the Army towards them, not knowing that my Lord *Inchiquin* might not be near with his Forces. But these Horse, when we were well in sight retired, whereupon Leiut. Gen. *Purcell* (with several other Officers and Gentlemen of the Country) who had been viewing them at near hand, came Galloping to me, saying that the Enemies were packing away, and pres'd me to let him have my Horse; for they had them so sure, that they could not possibly escape. I made some difficulty of the matter, but they said it was because I knew not the Country; yet I knew so much, that yielding to their desires, I should be exposed in a great Champaigne Country with an Army of Foot, and Cannon, without Horse. Nevertheless after all, (which I count certainly amongst other my Follies) I suffered my self to be perswaded, and they marched away with my Horse in great haft. I followed slowly, and coming to the *Blackwater*, near the Ford of *Fermoy*, drew my Foot and Cannon into an old *Danes* work; *Ireland* being full of them; and having stayed there a good while, and hearing no news of my Horse, I began to be uneasie. But

remem-

remembring that I had a Guard of Horse on some Beeves, that were for the Provision of the Army, I sent for them, and at the same time unexpected came to me *Garret Garrubh*, with my old Life-Guard of Horse out of *Leinster*; these, and those making in all about one hundred; having first ordered 1500 Foot to stand in a readiness, I marched with them to see what became of the Troops sent with *Purcell*; and finding by the Track, that my Horse had passed the Ford, and taken their way towards *Castle-Lyons*, I followed. Being come near the top of the Hill above the Ford, I left these few I had with me drawn up, and with some Officers went my self to a height to discover. Thence I saw all the Enemy formed in a great Plain with a Shrub wood before them, and my Horse in hast marching through to Charge, having with them 100. Commanded Foot. But the Enemy seeing the Squadrons broken, as they came on the Plain, gave them no time to form,

form, but Charged and defeated them. On sight of this disorder, and the Enemy pursuing, when they came near me, I advanced, crying out to my own men, that they should rally behind me. The Enemy seeing these fresh Horses, and not knowing but the Army might be near, pursued no further, but drew up. The 1500. Foot that I sent for, soon came to me; on sight of which the Enemy retiring to *Castle-Lyons*, I followed; but it being now dusky, could not engage them. Hence I marched to *Malloe*, and took it, but with some Shot of Cannon, and left a Garison in it. *Donerail* and *Liscarrol* made no resistance. *Milltowne* stood out, so that I thought it would cost some trouble. But whilst the Batteries were preparing, 2 or 3000. Boys belonging to the Army, that used to form themselves into Battalions, having got Crows of Iron, Pickaxes, and other Instruments, a little before Sun-set, fell on the Place; intending I suppose only to have taken the Cows

Cows and Sheep within a Court which was walled: but fuccefs carried them further; and with the help of fome Soldiers, they took the Caftle by ftrong hand. So all that fide of the *Black-water* being cleared, I fent the Army for fifteen days into Quarters of refrefhment, and I went my felf to *Killmallocke*, and other places, where I kept my Magazines. In the mean time my Lord *Inchiquin* having taken *Roftellan*, befieged *Ballymarter*, a Caftle belonging to his Uncle, *Edmund Fitzgerald* Senefchal of *Imokelle*. My Army being come together, I marched to fuccour it. But there being a flood in the *Black-water*, I was hindred for two days, fo that when I came in fight of the place, I found it taken and burning, and the Enemy retreating, fome to *Corke*, others to *Youghall*.

Having thus loft my Defign of fuccouring *Ballymartir*, and that which I wifh'd moft, engaging the Enemy, I ftay'd two or three days Encamped near this burnt Caftle, thinking what
to

to do. At length I got intelligence, that Col. *Henry O Bryan* Brother to the Lord *Inchiquin*, and Lieut. Col. *Courtney* with several other Officers were come by Boat to *Roſtellan*, to make merry; and that the Tide fallen their Boats were aground, and so would continue till high water. On the certainty of this I lost no time, but sent immediately a party to seize the Boats, lying more than a musquet-shot from the Castle, following as fast as I could with the Army. Which being come up, I presently fell to the work, planted my Guns on the Batteries made by my Lord *Inchiquin*, not yet destroyed, and in the morning the place yielded on discretion. Hence I marched to *Caſtle-Lyons*, which having after some Battery yielded, I advanced towards *Liſmore*. But *Coney-Caſtle* lying on a pass in my way, and sending on Summons a Defiance; I encamped before it, thinking to plant my Guns that night; but the Boys eased me of that trouble, and before it was dark took it, as they did the former,

former, by storm. Hence I wrote again to the Governor of *Lismore*, to put that place into my hands, that I might turn the Army another way, having as much kindness for the Owner as he could have; but not prevailing, I Invested it; and having ordered the Batteries left Leiut. Gen. *Purcell* to Command, and try if he could have better success with that place now than when he had formerly Besieged it; and so rode to *Killkenny*, as not willing to be present at the destruction of a house, where I formerly had received many Civilities. At my return five or six days after, I found the place yielded, and the Garison marching out. After this being encamped at *Tallow*, intelligence was brought me, that Collonel *Mac William Ridgeway* was gone from *Corke* into the County of *Limericke* with a great party of Horse and some Foot. I marched immediately with all my Horse, and 1500. Foot streight for *Corke*; coming near, I left my Foot to make good my retreat

treat, and about an hour in the night I arrived near the Gates, and put my self on the way to *Malloe*, by which *Mac William* was to return; and gently marching on, we met some of the Enemy, whom we Charged, and with little or no opposition, killed some and took others; but the night being extream dark, we could do no great Execution. In this blind scuffle Capt. *James Browne*, brother to Sir *Valentine Browne*, a brave Gentleman was slain. By the Prisoners we found that their Commander *Mac William Ridgeway* had been killed that day, shot out of a Castle in *Roches* Country. Which way they had taken to return with the Body, we could not find. We marched a little forwards; but it being so dark, that nothing could be done, I returned with my Party to *Tallow*, and marched the Army towards *Youghall*. All Castles on the way submitted on easie terms. I will only take notice of one, because of the accident, tho I have forgot

got the name of the place, I remember it was a Castle that yielded early in the morning without resistance. Now presently after it was surrendred, the weather being very fair, I went a hunting, leaving Col. *Henesey* to see the Quarter made good, which was to march with their Arms, Bag and Baggage. But the Soldiers having been used to take Places by strong hand, and so enriching themselves by Plunder, would have done the like by this, tho it had Conditions. To prevent this Out-rage, the Col. and several other Officers went into the Castle joyning with the Garrison in its defence. But the Foot nevertheless fell on, and great shooting there was on all sides; I wondred what the matter was, and fearing that the Lord *Inchiquin* had attempted something, I returned in great haft. The Soldiers seeing me come sooner than they expected, ran into the Woods adjoyning. When I came to the Castle, and Col. *Henesey* had related the matter, I made the Garrison

son march out according to their Conditions. Then I began to enquire after my Mutineers, and caused the Trumpets to sound and Drums to beat, for drawing all to their Arms: some time it was before these Gentlemen could be got together. And having at last put both Horse and Foot in order of Battel, I went from Battalion to Battalion, telling them their fault, and what the consequence might have been, and concluded that they all merited death. Which they acknowledging, I added that some Justice must be done, and asked them, whether they were content for example-sake, to deliver two out of each Battalion as it should fall amongst them by Lots? They agreed; but when they came to be shot, I thought the number too great, and made them throw again for two only, which suffered.

But to return to our Story; from this Castle I marched to *Youghall*, and Encamped loosely before it, thinking to distress the Place, and towards the Sea near *Crocker's* Works, I sent Major

Major General *Purcell* with 1500. men, and some small Pieces to hinder succour that might come by Sea. Whilst this was a doing, I went with a Party in the night, and two Pieces of Cannon and pass'd the *Blackwater* at *Temple Michaell*, and before day had my two Guns planted, at the Ferry point over against *Youghall*; and within less than Musquet-shot of two Parliament Frigats: at the second shot one blew up, but some days after the Enemy made a Sally from *Crocker*'s Works, and ill treated Major General *Purcell*, taking one of his Guns.

Now by way of digression, I must tell you that about this time, that is Midsummer 1645. arrived in the west of *Ireland Renuccini* Arch-Bishop and Prince of *Fermo*, in quality of *Nuncio* sent by Pope *Innocent* the tenth, to the Confederate Catholicks, and coming near the Coast was chased by a Parliament Frigat Commanded by one *Plunckett*; but as he was ready to lay him on Board, to the great misfortune

fortune of the Confederate Catholicks, and many other good Interests, *Pluncketts* Kitchin-Chimney took fire, which to quench he was forced to lye by, and give the *Nuncio* opportunity to gain the Shore.

Soon after this, there came a Fleet of Boats, and bigger Vessels sent by my Lord of *Inchiquin* from *Corke* with Supplies of men and Provision, and succoured the Town; on which I marched off, and trifled out the remain of that Campaigne in destroying the Harvest; only a Party of my men attempted to plunder the *great Island* near *Barryes Court*; but being ill guided in passing, and the Sea coming in sooner than they counted, their design failed. Besides there were of the Enemy that opposed their coming on dry Land, and Capt. *Thurlugh OBryan* was killed by a loose shot out of a Castle in the Island.

Now it being the latter end of *November*, the Snow falling, I retired to *Caperquin*, and Commissioners being come to lay out Winter-Quarters

ters for the Army, I left it and repaired to *Killkenny*, where I found the Council in great debate, and much divided oncerning the *Peace*, which their Commissioners had fully concluded with my Lord of *Ormond* at *Dublin*, and wanted nothing but to have their Agreements approved by the *Supream Council.* Many days the Dispute held after my coming to them; and at length, we that were for the Peace, finding our selves the greater number, pressed the putting it to the Vote; on which one of the contrary part, seeing it could not be refused, proposed that being we pretended all to be for the King, and differed only in the way of best serving him, to put us right we should do well to desire a certain *English Noble-man* then in Town, and lately come from *England*, to give us his Opinion in the matter, which he did in the afternoon absolutely against the *Peace*, if the *Nuncio* did not approve it; which was not to be hoped for. Thus all our endeavours that were

were for it came to nothing, and I for my part immediatly laid down my Commands of *Munster*, and would act no more.

Many reasons I had besides that drove me to despair; for tho on the first *Cessation*, if *Peace* had followed in any reasonable time, we might probably have kept up the King; yet now the matter was much changed, since the coming of the *Nuncio*, and *Inchiquin*'s Revolting with the *English* Army, and the Towns under his Command from the Kings Authority and declaring for the Parliament. This together with the underhand actings of the Earl of *Glamorgan*, newly come from *England*, gave much trouble to the Marquess of *Ormond*, in his endeavours for establishing the *Peace*. This L. of *Glamorgan*, pretending large Commissions from the King, by colour of which he had entred into several secret Treaties with the *Nuncio*'s Party, very contrary to what my Lord Lieutenant had been doing, gave such hopes to the *Confederates*,

derates, that they would give no ear to what the Lord Lieutenant had proposed. Besides, the Confederates since the arrival of the *Nuncio* had fallen into great Factions and Divisions, and amongst others began to renew the fatal distinction between the *old English* and *ancient Irish.*

On my quitting the Command of *Munster,* the Earl of *Glamorgan,* since made *Marquess of Worcester,* was chosen in my place, on promises that he would contribute out of his own purse great sums of Money towards the Service of the Province. In order to this he gave Commissions for the Raising many new Regiments, giving Winter-Quarters on the Province with promise of satisfaction: but my Lord *Inchiquin* towards the Spring, sent along by Sea from *Corke* 500. Foot and 150. Horsemen with Saddles and all sorts of Arms for Horse and Foot; and entring the *Shannon* seized *Bonratty* in the County of *Clare*; a Castle belonging to the Earl of *Thomond,* where they found a brave Stable of

Horses and Mares, on which he mounted all his Horsemen. The Earl of *Glamorgan*, to keep in this Garison, ordered some Troops to six-mile Bridge between *Limericke* and *Bonratty*, but were beaten by that Garison. The Earl, after this Rendezvouz'd his whole Army at *Clomnell*; to which Rendezvouz my Lord of *Muskry* came; and some Differences falling out between these two Noblemen, my Lord *Muskry* took the Command of the Army to himself, and with it Besieged *Bonratty*. To this Siege the *Supream Council* soon followed, the place held out five or six weeks; but not two days after, the Attack was changed to the side of the moorish Land towards the *Shannon*.

I must now tell you that the Lord *Inchiquin*, on the certainty of *Bonratty*'s being Besieged, and the whole Army of *Munster* engaged, marched into the County of *Limerick*, and having no Passage over the River of *Shannon* to go to its Succour, thought by by Diverſion to oblige my Lord *Muſkry* to draw off, by burning, plundring, and deſtroying the Country even to the Gates of *Limerick*.

In this City the *Supream Council* ſate at that time, whither I coming by chance they ſent for me, and having ſufficiently declared to me the ill condition they were in, (for Sir *Charles Coot* was acting in *Connaught* the ſame part that my Lord of *Inchiquin* played in *Munſter*) they deſired my Aſſiſtance, and prayed that I would head ſome Horſe they had appointed to Rendezvouz near *Cloghnotfye*, a Houſe of Sir *Edmond Fitzharris* ſeated in the Mountain that runs between the Counties of *Corke* and *Limerick*. Theſe were but 500. old Horſe commanded by *mac Thomas*, the reſt, which they reckon'd 1500. more, were to conſiſt of Gentlemen and ſuch as they brought with them: I excuſed my ſelf as well as I could, alledging, that ſince my quitting the Command in *Munſter*, I had laid aſide all thoughts of War, and

that

that I came there as a Passenger in my way to see the Siege of *Bonratty*, having neither Equipage nor Horse for Service. But on their promises to furnish me with these and other necessaries, I was at length overcome by their perswasions or rather pity of their Condition. My condescention was immediately published for the encouragement of the Gentry; and the next day I went to the Rendenzvouz, where I found the 500. Horse with *Mac Thomas*, and as many Gentlemen with their Dependents, as made 500. more, which I immediately formed into Squadrons, and drew against my Lord *Inchiquin*, and kept as near him as I durst; so that now he Marched and Encamped pretty close. This lasted four or five days, till at length my Lord *Inchiquin*, finding this Check hindred him from destroying the Country, retired to his Garisons; and I went to the Siege. All this while a Treaty of *Peace* with my Lord of *Ormond* went on, tho much opposed by the

Nuncio

Nuncio and the *National Congregation of the Clergy* gathered by his orders at *Waterford*, where they met the other four Arch-Bishops, and most of the Bishops and Heads of Religious Orders in the Kingdom. The *Nuncio* and this Congregation went so far as to declare the Confederate Commissioners treating with my Lord Lieutenant, and all others that should submit unto the Peace in hand, perjur'd and forsworn, threatning them with Thunders of Excommunication in case of persisting. This with some secret Concessions they had gained from the Earl of *Glamorgan* in favor of their Religion, not discovered till found in the Arch-Bishop of *Tuam*'s pocket after he was killed in a fight near *Sligo*, divided the Confederate Catholicks into two Factions, the one called the *Nuncio*'s, the other *Ormond*'s Party. Yet notwithstanding, the Treaty went on, and concluded in an agreement called the Peace of 46. which being proclaimed at *Killkenny* the Lord Lieutenant came thither

thither accompanied with many Noble-men and others besides 1200. Foot, and 200. Horse as a Guard. The *Supreme Council* received him with all due respect and surrendred their Government to him. But this Sun-shine lasted not long, when the news was brought that those of *Limerick* had rejected the Peace, declaring for the Pope's *Nuncio*, and affronted the King at Arms, going to Proclaim it; that *Clomnell* shut their Gates on the same score. General *Owen Roe ONeale* being proud of a late Victory, he had gained over the *Scots* in *Ulster*, declared also for the Popes *Nuncio*. *Preston*, General of *Leinster*, being at *Birrh* in the Kings County, looked very cloudily, yet held correspondence with my Lord Lieutenant, but withal excusing his attendance on pretence of some Indisposition.

 The Nuncio now being at *Waterford*, in the head of the mentioned Congregation, and having by his Threats of Excommunications thus broken

broken us, the Lord Lieutenant by advice of the Commissioners of Trust, (which were men named by the Confederates to see the Peace observed) sent me to try if I could perswade the *Nuncio* to let the Peace go on. But all I could do was in vain, he declaring his Resolution to oppose it to the uttermost, with other expressions relating to Blood, not becoming a Church-man.

Being returned, and having acquainted my Lord Leiutenant with what had passed, and seeing him still fixed to his design of marching into *Munster*, I was something troubled; and finding Col. *John Barry* a man in much credit with his Excellency at Sir *Lucas Dillon*'s Lodgings, I discovered to them my apprehensions concerning my Lord Lieutenants intended march into *Munster*; by setting forth the malice I found in the Clergy-Party, and how they grew daily stronger by the Revolt of Troops and Towns unto them; that *Owen ONeale* was a declared Enemy, and

at

at the head of a Victorious Army, and might certainly if we marched further cut our retreat; that my Lords Party for number were not confiderable, and that the *Supreme Council* were diffolved on the Proclamation of the *Peace*, and confequently of no Authority to make good the publick Faith; with much more to this effect, concluding the march very dangerous.

They promifed to difcourfe this with my Lord Lieutenant; but whether they did or no, or if they did, whether his Excellency would believe fo much falfhood to be amongft Men, as was then defigning againft him, I cannot tell; but in two or three days after, he began his March for *Munfter*, and coming to *Carrick*, a Houfe of his own, word was brought him there, that *Mac Thomas* had declared for the *Nuncio*, and was drawn up near *Clomnell* with three or four hundred Horfe. I was fent to him by his Excellency, as thinking my Intereft might have gained
fomething

something on him, becaufe he had ferved moft of the Wars under my Command. When I came, and delivered him my Meffage, he anfwered that he was engaged with the *Nuncio* according to his Confcience, and would not quit him. I acquainted his Excellency with this anfwer, and added, that I faw no hopes of reclaiming this man; yet my Lord Leiutenant went on, and took his way towards *Cafhell*; *Mac Thomas* Marching for the moft part in fight of us. As we came near the Town, and made fome halt, his Excellency received advice, I think from my Lord *Dillon*, refiding at *Afhlone*, that *ONeale* was marching againft him with all the Force he could make; whereupon my Lord was pleafed to call me to him, and telling me his intelligence asked my opinion, what was beft to be done. I gave it quickly, that he fhould immediately march back the fhorteft way, and indeavour to gain *Laughlin-Bridge*. This he did accordingly, but paffing near

Kill-

Killkenny he sent his Brother Sir *George Hanbleton* and my self to let the Magistrates of that City know what Intelligence he had from all hands; however, if they pleased he would come to them, with the Party he had, and venture his Fortune with them. They received the Message with all due respect, and answered, that if he pleased to come to them, they would serve him with their Lives and Fortunes, tho they did believe it would be the loss of him and them together. On our report his Excellency kept on for the gaining of *Laughlin,* where there was a Bridge that crossed the River *Barroe,* a Fort at the end, on the County of *Catharloe's* side Commanded by Col. *Walter Bagnall.* Having gained this Point, we lost no time in our March to *Dublin,* where coming near, I think the whole People of the City came forth to meet his Excellency, with as much joy as ever Man was received, having for several days judged him and his Party lost. As we we came into the Suburbs, his Excellency honoured me with the carrying of the Sword before him through the City, for which I can give no other Reason (besides his own goodness) but that I had been always a promoter of the *Peace,* and the only Man of the Confederate Catholicks, that came with him, and never left him in these his Adventures.

The *Nuncio* now thought all his own, Committed to Prison such of the late *Supreme Council* and others as he called of *Ormonds* Party, and having got his Forces together, Commanded by *ONeale* and *Preston* as Generals under him, he Marched them in one Army, (tho for their better conveniency they took two different ways) towards *Dublin*; they were noised so numerous, and so Powerful, that in good earnest the People, Officers, and Soldiers did not know what to make of it, and shewed apprehension enough. His Excellency perceiving this, as it was too plain, called for me and we discoursed

scoursed the whole matter. I took the boldness to give my Opinion, which was, That this Army of the *Nuncio* could no longer subsist in any place than they found Provisions where they came; that neither of these Generals had any Magazines during the War; that they undertook this matter in confidence of the plenty they should find in his Quarters; that I thought it was a thing of too great hazard to oppose them in the Field, and yet if they were not stoped, they would come on, and at least live upon him till they had eaten all; Lastly, that on consideration of the whole, I thought it best to prevent their coming too near; which could not be done by any other way than by destroying the Quarters. His Excellency was of the same opinion, and therefore sent orders immediately to all people within eight miles of the Town to bring in whatever they had, giving them three or four days time for it, and what was found abroad after the time prefixed,

parti-

particularly Forage and Mills, Parties were ordered to burn and destroy them. This was all effected before the *Nuncio* and his Army were come to *Killkallin Bridge.* Yet notwithstanding this discouragement they advanced as far as *Leixlipp* and *New-Castle*; both which places lying within three miles distant one of another, and six from *Dublin*; They made their Head Quarters, *Preston* at *Leixlipp* and *Owen ONeale* at *New-Castle,* the *Nuncio* with his Council remaining at *Seginstown* some six miles further off. But not being able to live long on the air; for from their own Countrys they expected not much, and the continual Rains having raised the River of *Liffy,* and all the Bridges being broken hindred what was coming to them: and great Jealousies (even more than the ordinary old ones) arising 'twixt the two Generals, and 'twixt the *Nuncio* also and *Preston,* they return'd several ways in greater haste than they came.

The

The Quarters being destroyed, and *Athlone* betrayed to the *Nuncio* by *Dillon* a Fryar, and the Harbor of *Dublin* block'd up by Parliament Men of War, the Marquess of *Ormond* was forced to treat: and of the two chose to apply himself to the Parliament of *England*: during which Treaty his Excellency was forced to march into the County of *Westmeathe* and other parts to feed his People, where we were not much at our ease, for *Owen ONeale* continually Alarm'd us.

Now all being agreed for the Delivery of the places under the Marquess's Command to the *Parliament Commissioners*, of which Mr. *Annesley* since made Earl of *Anglesey*, was chief, I took my leave of his Excellency, resolving to go to *France*, tho with much grief of heart to leave this Noble Lord, who had shewed so much Loyalty, Justice, and Steddiness in his Proceedings, during these Transactions, even from the meeting in *Seginstowne* to the conclusion of the *Peace* made with

with the *Confederates,* and now again to the giving up of his Government to the Parliament, for which I doubt not but he shall remain in Story, as he deserves, a fixed Star, by whose Light others may walk in his steps; this was the effect of breaking the *Peace* of 46. And let the failure of that *Peace* lye at whose door it will, 'tis no rashness to say, that Story hardly mentions any one thing that had so fatal a Consequence. For if this *Peace* had gone on, the King had presently been supplied with great Forces out of *Ireland* both of *English* and *Irish:* and probably might have prevented the ensuing mischiefs that shortly after hapned, both to him and to all his Loyal Subjects throughout his Dominions.

But the *Irish* had a more particular ill fate than the rest by this breach of Faith; ☞ for albeit they discovering their Error, did, not long after mightily endeavor to make amends the best they could by a second and very solemn agreement, called the *Peace* of 48. which their Commissioners signed, and themselves confirmed and Sealed with the Blood of many ☞ thousands of their best men, who lost their Lives to maintain it, refusing in the mean time advantageous offers of *Peace* (and that even to the very last) made to them by the *Parliament*; yet since his Majesty's most happy Restauration, all their Estates some very few excepted, do by the Act of Settlement remain with the Conquerers.

☞ The Marquess of *Ormond* having performed Agreements with the *Parliament*, left *Ireland*, and after some time spent in *England*, went for *France*. At St. *Germans* he attended the Queen and Prince of *Wales*. But it was not long before my Lord *Inchiquin*, having some discontent given him by the *Parliament* entred into secret Treaties with the Lord *Taaff*, since made Earl of *Carlingford*, and other Principal Leaders amongst the well-affected *Irish*, who since the rejection of the *Peace* had lost two great

great Battels, the one at *Dungans Hill* at *Linchs Knock*, under General *Prston*, the other at *Knocknanoss* under my Lord *Taaff*; and looking on these great Losses on their side, as heavy Judgments of Heaven to punish the late unparallelled breach of Faith, they began to be as weary of the *Nuncio*, as my Lord *Inchiquin* was of the *Parliament*. (Wherefore, after some time spent in Treaties between them, both Parties concluded a Cessation of Arms. The *Nuncio* then at *Killkenny* did what he could to hinder this *Cessation*, but not prevailing, retir'd in discontent to *Kilminchin* in the *Queens County*, a Country intirely possessed by *ONeales* Troops, who had Fortified *Athy*, the *Fort of Lease*, and all other places capable of strength, and provided what was needful. Yet the *Nuncio*, for all his haste out of *Killkenny*, did not omit to leave behind him an Interdict on all places, and an Excommunication against all persons that should adhere to the Cessation of Arms made with my Lord *Inchiquin*. But feeing this had no great effect, after a time he left *Killminchin* and went to *Gallway*; where finding the Townfmen for the moft part approving the Ceffation, he put an Interdict on the Churches and Chappels there, caufing the Doors to be fhut up; but the Arch-Bifhop of *Tuam* got them to be opened by Force, which caufed fuch a Buftle that a man or two were killed in the tumult.

 The *Irifh* and *Inchiquin's* Party thus now in Ceffation of Arms, they concluded to contrive the Marquefs of *Ormond's* return, and upon his Arrival to Declare for the King. To this end Agents were fent from the Confederates to *France*, *viz.* the Marquefs of *Antrim*, the Lord Vifcount *Muskry*, and *Jeoffry Browne* Efquire, who acted fo effectually, that upon their offers the Queen and Prince of *Wales* difpatched my Lord Lieutenant for *Ireland*, and accordingly he fhipt at *Haver de Grace* in a States Man of War, and landed at
Corke,

Cork, my self and many others attending him. My Lord *Inchiquin* was then with his Army in the Field, but came to him in a short time. I went before to *Killkenny*, whither his Excellency came soon after, and a new Treaty was set on Foot between him and an Assembly of the *Irish* then sitting in Town. But the matter being of great weight, the Assembly used all means to be rightly informed of their Condition, and therefore required the Bishop of *Ferns*, and Sir *Nicholas Plunckett*, lately return'd from *Rome*, to declare faithfully what might be expected from the *Pope* and Court of *Rome*; they very ingeniously gave an account of all that passed in the Negotiation with the *Pope*, and his Ministers, concluding that no Assistance or Supplys were to be expected from that side. Hereupon the Assembly named commissioners to draw up such Articles as might be proposed to my Lord Lieutenant in order to a *Peace*. After some days his Excellency and the Commissioners came to a full agreement, which the Assembly approved, and it goes by the name of the Peace of 1648. What Agreement there was Between his Excellency and my Lord *Inchiquin*, I know not; but am sure that *Inchiquin* demanded of my Lord Lieut. and obtained all *Munster* for the recruiting and strengthening his Army. The Peace of 48. thus Concluded, the *Nuncio* Shipp'd himself for *France*, and so to his own Country after he had broken the *Confederacy*, and imprisoned most of the *Supream Council*, with others, that would not submit unto him; and also had been the Cause of shedding the Blood of many thousands slain in fighting his Battels and Parties; all which concluded with the Extirpation of the *Irish* Nation together with the Destruction of the Catholick Religion in that Kingdom. And the satisfaction the Confederates got by this disorder was the *Nuncio*'s confinement to his Arch-Bishoprick after the Pope had checked him with these words only, *you,*

you behaved your self rashly. From the Excommunication the *Supream Council* and Assembly in behalf of themselves and the whole Nation, appealed to the Pope and so it remaineth to this day.

But to my own Story, I am to tell you that in the *Peace* of 46. there was an Article by which it was left to the Confederate Catholicks to name certain persons for general Officers, to whom my Lord Lieutenant was to give Commissions.

Now I having served them long as has been seen, and the same Article being confirmed in this Peace of 48. they named me, as they had done in the former, to be General of the Horse of the whole Kingdom, which his Excellency approved of, gave me his Commission accordingly, and soon after sent me into the *Queens County* with 5000. Foot and 1000. Horse, with some Cannon to reduce the *Fort of Lease*, otherwise called *Mary Borough Athy* and other Garisons, possessed

sed by *ONeals* People. Those Troops for the most part were Commanded by Sir *Thomas Armstrong*, Col. *Treswell*, and other *English* Officers, men that had always followed my Lord Lieutenants Fortune; and had been recruited and reinforced out of their Winter-Quarters at *Killkenny* and some Counties about it. With these having well executed my Order and reduced those Garisons, I marched to *Laughlin Bridge*, and there Encamped, giving an account to his Excellency of what had passed, and that I would expect there his farther Orders. But I was not many days, before my Lord Lieutenant, the Lord *Inchiquin* Lieutenant General of the Army, the Lord *Taaff* Master of the Ordnance, Mr. *Daniel ONeale* Governor of his Excellencies Guards of Horse, with other Generals and the whole Army of my Lord *Inchiquins* and some *Irish* Regiments joyned us. With this Army, and a good Train of Artillery, we passed the River *Barrow*, and that night Encamped in in the County of *Catharloe*, where something passed in point of Command, that gave me ground to judge my self not well dealt with, besides I was harassed by my Marches and Labours in the *Queens County*. In Consideration of which his Excellency at my request gave me leave to retire for some days to refresh my self, and his Excellency Marched on and invested *Dublin*.

I returned to *Killkenny*, where being arrived, I found the whole City in an uproar; the Occasion, and Issue of it, take as followeth. One Father *Caron*, at that time Commissary General of the *Recollects* all over *Ireland*, being in *Killkenny* to reform the Abuses of his Order there, was by the Commissioners of Trust desired to remove one *Brenan* and six or seven more out of the *Franciscan* Monastery of that Town, and send them elsewhere to be kept under Discipline; their reason was, that these men were notoriously known to be still most violent sticklers for the ways of
the

the *Nuncio*, and that they made it their bufinefs to incenfe the People anew againft the *Peace*, to alienate them from the Government and draw them wholly to *Owin ONeale*, who yet ftood out againft all agreement with the King.

To fatisfie fo juft a demand of the Commiffioners, Father *Caron* appoints a day for *Brenan* and his Affociates to depart *Killkenny*, and go to the feveral other Convents, which he had appointed for them. And becaufe he found by their anfwers they were refolved not to obey him, the *Commiffioners of Truft*, upon notice thereof, more effectually refolved to force their Obedience to his Commands, by fending them away conducted by Guards, (yet by Guards of Roman-Catholick-Soldiers) to the Convents appointed them by their Superior.

On this refolution of the *Commiffioners of Truft*, *Brenan* and his refractory Brothers having timely notice, and feeing no remedy, but by the Intereft tereſt they had in the Town, three or four of them being Natives, as one by name *Rooth*, was Brother to the Maior; beſides confiding in the Common People, whom they had already poſſeſſed with many Lies, but above all perſwading themſelves that no Catholick durſt attempt to violate the Sanctity of their Habit, or the priviledge of their Profeſſion by laying violent hands upon them; and Proteſtants they knew very well there were none in Town. What do they conclude at laſt? even very Religiouſly to raiſe dangerous Tumults, and that by a moſt falſe and malicious Invention.

When the day appointed was come, theſe unruly Regulars, by themſelves and their Emiſſaries, inform the heads of the Rabble abroad, that the Commiſſary and Father *Peter Walſh*, with ſome five or ſix more of their Company, had privately introduced a number of my Lord *Inchiquin*'s Proteſtant *Iriſh* Soldiers, into their Convent and cloathed them like Friars

ars, of purpose to seize at night those few Religious men that remained unalterable in their obedience, to the *See Apostolicke*; and either to draw them into the River *Neoir*, that ran by their Garden, or waft them over by Boat, and put them to a more cruel death elsewhere, in some unknown place.

This lie did so enflame the meaner sort in the Town, and Suburbs, (already pretty well prepared by many other inventions) that upon a sudden, many of them forced their way into the Monastery, cursing and exclaiming against those that would turn away their friends.

Then arming themselves with what came next to their hands, with all Fury imaginable they attacked a little Castle, whereinto the Commissary with his Company withdrew, to save themselves. At this time I came to Town, accompanied by Sir *George Hamilton* and four or five Gentlemen, with about a dozen Horse, three Trumpets, and some Footmen; and being

being informed of the matter, I Galloped presently with those of my Company to the place, had a Charge Sounded, and fell among the Rabble, and Firing of Pistols, and Crying, Kill, Kill, Kill. The multitude hearing the Trumpets, and seeing the Fire, (for 'twas now grown dusky) and knowing my voice, were surprized, and thought themselves betrayed, as knowing the Army to be far off, in their March to *Dublin*, and therefore immediately routed, and ran away; tho they had brought them in the Castle so low, that to speak within compass, they could not hold out a quarter of an hour. The Fathers being thus relieved, after four hours defence, I enquired who governed this Siege, and found that seven or eight Friars of the Convent, and above all the aforementioned, *Brenan*, and *Rooth* were the chief contrivers of this Tumult. I sent for these Incendiaries, and whilst I was reasoning with them, the Town Major one *Archer*, with an hundred

hundred Musqueteers came to my affiftance, and prefently followed the Mayor, and Aldermen; whom after I had roundly ratled for fuffering this diforder, I commanded them to lay hold of thofe Friars, and carry them Prifoners to the Caftle. At which they ftaggering, and this *Brenan*, a fturdy Friar prefuming to fay, he would fain fee what man durft touch his Habit, I laid hold on him, faying *lies the Enchantment there?* and then the Mayor, Town Major, and the reft carried them away Prifoners to the Caftle as I had ordered.

Now after a while that I had diverted my felf with hunting, and other recreations in the Country, I repaired to *Limmerick*; and while I ftaid there, I caufed all the People of that City, and County (either by fair, or foul means) to bring in what remained due to the King of their Applotment and got together about ten thoufand pounds, which I delivered to Sir *George Hamilton* Treafurer of the Army. My Lord Lieutenant now

now wrote to the *Commissioners of Trust*, sitting at *Killkenny*, to let me know, that I should now come to the Army, and all difficulties concerning Command should be removed, to my satisfaction. I obeyed, and Sir *George Hamilton* and my self with our ten thousand pounds, went streight to the Army, which we found in their March removing from the *Phœnix*-side of *Dublin* to *Rathmines* where they Encamped.

But my Lord *Inchiquin* soon after acquainted his Excellency, with some Letters he had received from his Officers in *Munster*, that *Cromwell* was to land in that Country; which if true, he feared all his Towns would Revolt, if not prevented by his speedy repair thither, with all or at least the most part of his Army; and desired his Excellencies consent, that he might march away with 1100. Horse, to secure the Province. This his Excellency imparted to me, which surprised me extremely, being sure the whole was Army too weak for the

the work in hand. Neverthelefs my Lord *Inchiquin* Marched away with his 1100. Horfe, and you may imagine, many more; which in great meafure, gave way to the Defeat, that foon after hapned before *Dublin*.

Not long after this, *Cromwell*, with his Army Landed at *Dublin*, Marched to *Tredath*, and took it (with all the Towns in them parts) by Storm; and thofe within, near 3000. men, he put all to the Sword. My Lord Lieutenant being not able to make head againft him retired with what Troops he had to the County of *Kilkenny*, where my Lord *Inchiquin* came to him, and in a fhort time made up a pretty good Army; for befides my Lord *Inchiquins* Forces, many *Ulfter* Regiments of Foot joyned them; *Owen ONeale*, having by this time (tho too late for himfelf and the Kings Service) come in upon Articles, which he figned upon his Death-Bed, after he had been rejected by the Parliament.

Crom-

Cromwell having thus carried all before him about *Tredath*, returned to *Dublin*, to refresh his Army; yet staid not many days, but took his March by the Sea side, through the County of *Wicklow* to besiege *Wexford*. My Lord *Inchiquin* was sent to oppose; and met him on the strand toward *Glascarrigg* in the County of *Wexford*, and fought him, but was defeated.

My Lord Lieutenant being with his Army come to *Rosse*, and fearing that *Wexford* now Besieged, was not sufficiently manned to hold out, till he had got an Army together, to raise the Siege, or fight *Cromwell*; I, as knowing the Town and Country about it, offered to attempt the Relief of it. His Excellency accepted of my good Will, and ordered me as many Regiments of *Ulster* Foot, as made one thousand five hundred men, and appointed 200 Horse to escort us. I took a great compass and came before day to the Ferry, near Sir *Thomas Esmonds* House, called *Ballintreman*, *tremtan*, who as I remember was along with me upon this Expedition. Then leaving the Horse for my return, I pass'd that Arm of the Sea in Boats, and having delivered the Foot to Sir *Edmund Butler* (the Governor) I took the same way homewards as I came.

The Town, thus manned was Impregnable as to *Cromwell* by Force; yet he took it by the advantage of a Castle that was betrayed unto him, by the Governor *James Stafford*. This Castle was strong, and stood about 3 or 400 paces from the Wall. The Communication with the Town could not be cut, so that the danger was least there, if Treachery had not been in the case. But the Castle being betrayed, it mastered all that part of the wall, whereupon *Cromwell's* Forces entred and made almost as great a slaughter as at *Droghedae*.

My Lord Lieutenant then with his Army retired over the River of *Rosse*, and Encamped on the County of *Killkenny's* side; from whence his Excellency

lency sent me into the County of *Waterford*, to *Passage*, over against *Ballyhack*, to look after the relieving of *Duncannon*, Besieged by some of *Cromwell*'s People. I think *Ireton* commanded; and for all there were Parliament Ships before it, I ventured one morning with a Boat, and got into the place to the Governor, a brave Gentleman one Col. *Wogan*, whom my Lord sometime before had sent thither to Command, and with him besides the *Irish* Garison about 100 *English* Officers, who had served the King in the Wars of *England*. This Gentleman from the highest part of the Rampier shewed me how the Enemy lay, and after I had well considered all, I offered to send him that night by Sea 80 Horses, with Saddles and Pistols, if he could mount them with so many of his *English* Officers, and before day make a sharp Sally with them, and some Foot upon the Enemy. He liked the proposal extremely, but doubted much my performance; it being about three miles by Sea. I desired

desired him to leave that Town, and assured him, he should shortly be satisfied of what I undertook.

Having thus concluded, I took my Boat, returned, and immediately set my self to my business, that I might lose no time because the Tide served in the beginning of the night. And having provided Boats, I commanded 80 Horse, to come to the Sea-side, caused them to be Boated out of hand, and sent them away. They came all to *Duncannon* safe, and undiscovered, and all was executed as designed, great slaughter made, and the Cannon seized; for the confusion amongst the Enemy was great, by reason that they judged it the falling in of an Army from abroad, seeing Horses come against them, and knowing of none in the Fort: our people retiring before day, the Enemy raised the Siege in the Morning, and Marched off.

His Excellency after this, made me Governor of *Waterford*; whither I went in with 1000 men; but the
Town

Town would not admit them entrance. Whereupon after several days dispute, despairing of success, I marched away in the night: All this while the Armies were not idle; for *Cromwell* after the Rendition of *Wexford* came to *Rosse*, and making a Breach took it. There he passed the River, and marched through the County of *Killkenny* to *Carrick*, and crossing the River of *Shuir* into the County of *Waterford*, marched on into the County of *Corke*, where all my Lord *Inchiquin*'s Towns opened their Gates to him. But *Cromwell* for his better security left Col. *Reynolds*, with a great party of Horse, and Foot in *Carrick* to keep the Town and Bridg which is over the River *Shuir*. Towards the Evening my Lord Lieutenant came to this place with his Army, but before he attempted any thing, was called away, on an alarm, that *Waterford* was in danger; and left the Command of his Army to my Lord *Inchiquin* and Lord *Taaff*, who immediately gave order to Storm the Place.

Place. This was done with great Valour, but wanting materials to make a Breach in the Wall, or to Scale it, they were after some hours forced to draw off, having lost some hundreds of men. I was present at this Action, but few knew it. The more particular actings of the Armies, I must leave to the Relation of those that know better, for I was seldom with them, but employed up and down, as you see. The persons principally intrusted by my Lord Lieutenant, for the Government of the Army, were my Lord *Inchiquin*, and my Lord *Taaffe* till the Spring following.

Then *Cromwell* began to move again, having drawn his Forces together, and had gained one Captain *Tickle* to secure him a Gate or two of *Killkenny*, and to betray into his hands, my Lord Lieutenant, my self, and some others, when he should think fit. The Plague strangely raged there at that time, as it had for a long while in our Towns thereabouts

bouts; and *Cromwell* having left his Garisons in the County of *Cork* in good order, was advanced into the County of *Tipperary*, in his way to the Siege of *Killkenny*; I having nothing to do went early one morning a Fox-hunting, as I was accustomed all the Winter. My Lord Lieutenant joyning me said, he would see what we did, and being a little further out of Town, he began to tell me how he had discovered the Treachery of *Tickle*, *Cromwell's* approach, and his design to Besiege this City. After some discourse, it was not long before my Lord came to the point, and told me it was resolved in Council, that he should immediately repair into the County of *Clare*, and from thence and the adjacent Countries endeavour the raising of an Army, to attend the motions of *Cromwell*; and that in his absence he should appoint me Commander in chief of the Province in *Leinster*.

Any man may judge how I was pleased with this Honour; but my obedience

bedience (tho I thought my self loft by it) obliged me to a submission, and caft my felf at my Lords feet to difpofe of me as he pleafed: The Commiffioner with all neceffary Orders difpatched his Excellency with his Generals, and *Commiffioners of Truft*, left *Killkenny*, and went ftrait to the County of *Clare*.

I loft no time in this juncture, but beftirr'd my felf with all poffible diligence, making Major *James Walfh*, Governor of the Caftle, and Sir *Walter Butler* of the City; and having done all I could to furnifh it with Men, Provifion, and Ammunition of all forts, I marched out my felf, leaving the Garifons about 200 Horfe, and 1000 Foot ftrong.

Cromwell now moving from *Cafhell*, on his March to *Callen*, I went to *Catherlogh*, hoping to have met there fuch Troops, from all parts of the Province, as I had ordered; but was difappointed; for thofe Quartered in the higher part of the divident, under the Command of the Lord *Dillon*,

lon, intirely failed, being about the number of 2500 Foot, and 6 or 700 Horse, and in their stead I received a Letter from his Lordship, as if he were sending them in great haft, but they never came, tho I repeated often my Orders.

These and some other Troops not appearing, I knew not well what to do; for I had but 800 Foot of the Province, and an *Ulster* Regiment of 1200 more. Sir *Thomas Armstrong* Commissary General of the Horse, was with me, and his Regiment with my Lord Lieutenant's Commanded by Col. *Treswell*, and some other Troops made up near 1000 Horse. At this time an *Irish man* was brought unto me, taken by some of my Guards, who being to be examined, desired to speak to me alone; which being granted, he produced a piece of yellow Wax, in form almost round, which he was to swallow on occasion, within it there was a Note from Col. *Hewson* to *Cromwell*, intimating, that he with his Forces, were upon their March

March from *Dublin*, but desired his Orders, in respect that I lay in his way. Having copied the Note, I rolled it in the Wax as I had it; and the Fellow having assured me of his return with *Cromwell's* answer, I let him go on his way. Within two or three days after, he returned, and delivered me another piece of Wax, as the former with *Cromwell's* Orders to *Hewson* inclosed, which I kept; however *Hewson* held on his March, and passed the River *Barrow*, eight or ten miles below me.

Now tho I was not of strength to meddle with any of these Armies, yet I made some advantage of my intelligence: For whilst they were joyning, I marched to *Athy*, a Town with a Bridge eight miles above me, on the same River, where *Hewson* had a Magazine, with 700 men in Garison, and coming before it an hour before sun-set, I took it by Storm, with all the Garison Prisoners, at discretion. But the Place not being tenable, I slighted it, and not knowing what

what to do with my Prisoners, I made a Present of them to *Cromwell*, desiring him, (by Letter) to do the like to me, if any of mine should fall into his power.

But he little valued my Civility, for in a very few days after, he Besieged *Gowran* where Col. *Hammond* Commanded, and the Soldiers Mutining, and giving up the Place, with their Officers, he caused *Hammond* with some other *English* Officers, to be shot to death. And having thus gained *Gowran* and cleared all other places in the County, he fell to work, and Besieged the very Town of *Killkenny*. Whereupon I took my March to *Bally raggett*, within seven miles of him. But finding my self too much exposed there, I Marched to *Ossory*, and made my Head-Quarter in *Castle-Town*, a place belonging to Mr. *Fitz-Patrick*; whence I sent to the Lord *Dillon* to come to me with all the Force he had. He gave me still fair promises, (as before) but never came. Then with the advice of Sir
Thomas

Thomas Armstrong and Col. *Treswell,* I resolved with my Party, to enter *Killkenny,* which was easie to be done, the side where the River runs, being open. But when I came to my Rendezvouz, my *Ulster* Regiment appeared not, but were Marched away to their own Country; alledging they came to Fight against men, but not against God; their meaning was because of the Plague.

This design being thus broken, and a great Breach made in the Wall near the Castle, which had been assaulted two or three times, and no hopes ever to be succoured, I sent orders to the Governor to make conditions, when they thought fit, and both to joyn at the same time, tho the Castle might hold out two or three days longer than the Town.

Cromwell being thus Master of *Killkenny,* I retired into the Kings County; where understanding that *Carloe* Castle was Besieged, I appointed a Rendezvouz, intending to attempt the Succour; but coming to the place, I found

I found not half my Foot, the reſt were marched into *Munſter*, I know not by whoſe Orders.

Now finding my ſelf thus uſed, and reflecting on ſome other hardſhips, put upon me ſince the *Peace* of 1648. in deſpair of ſucceſs, I left *Leinſter*, and went to my Lord Lieutenant in the County of *Clare*, where I rendred him an account how I had been diſappointed, to the end he might do as he thought fit.

I had not been long there attending his Excellency, before *Ireton* ſate down before *Limrick* on the County of *Limrick*-ſide, leaving *Thomond*'s ſide open. His Excellency repaired thither, and being come near the end of the Bridge, ſent to the Mayor to let him know he was there with ſome Troops, and ready to enter with them, for the defence of the place. The Mayor having conſulted his Brethren made excuſe, as if they had no need of Relief. Several Meſſages paſſed to and fro, till at length his Excellency loſing all patience, declared unto them,

that

that if they would not receive and obey him, he would leave the Kingdom. But seeing all would not do, he called me aside, and told me, he was in good earnest, and would be gone; but commanded me to stay, and keep up a Bustle as long as I could, it being the Kings Service. I was very unwilling to stay behind, seeing he took with him, my Lord *Inchiquin*, my Lord *Taaffe*, Col. *Daniel ONeale*, and other his friends. But the sound of the Kings Service, so charmed me, that I abandoned my own Judgment, and submitted to what his Excellency should order. He then gave me a Commission to be Commander in Chief of the Province of *Munster*, and the County of *Clare*, having already that of *Leinster*, and of the General of the Horse of the whole Kingdom. Thus qualified, his Excellence gave me possession of his Troops there in their Arms, together with his Life-Guards, to serve me, as they had done him, in all about 2000 Foot, and 1000 Horse.

His

His Excelleny for my better encouragement, assured me that he would leave a Commission for my Lord *Clanrickard* to be Lord Deputy.

Now my Lord being gone, and not suffering me to accompany him more than a mile, I went into the Town addressing my self to the Mayor and Aldermen, and I told them how I was left, and asked them whether they were pleased with it, or would obey me in that Station? They took some time to consult; but at length submitted to my pleasure. Whereupon immediately I visited their Walls, and at the same time took a view of the Enemy, whom I judged to be very loose, and exposed, if vigorously assaulted: and therefore resolved, in the beginning of the night to draw my Troops into Town, and a little before day, to make a sharp Sally. On what Intelligence I know not, but *Ireton* raised his Siege, and marched off that very night. This done, I returned my Troops to their Quarters, and remained my self in the Town, till

till I had sent orders to all Officers, commanding in the several Provinces, and particularly to my Lord *Muskry*, then in *Kerry*, whom I desired to make himself as strong as he could, and that I would soon be with him, to increase his Forces. In order to this I passed the *Shannon*, in the night about twelve miles below *Limrick*, with 2000 men; and tho the River was full of Parliament Ships, and two miles over, yet I had not the least loss, but landed safe in *Kerry*, near *Drumbeg*, took *Lestole*, and Marched till I came to my Lord *Muskry*'s at *Tralee*. Having acquainted his Lordship with what had passed, and ordered what I would have done, particularly in raising of Forces, I left my men with him, and returned to *Innis* my Residence in the County of *Clare*.

From thence, after some refreshment, I went to *Portumna*, to visit the Marquess of *Clanrickard* who bid me very welcome. After Dinner I desiring to retire my self for an hour or or two, he brought me to my Chamber, and asked whether it would not be troublefom, that he ftaid a little with me? I anfwered no, but the contrary; for my point was to get him to take the Government, by accepting the Commiffion left by my Lord Lieutenant; yet I fpake nothing of it, hoping that he would begin; which he did. The paffages on this Subject are too tedious to be related; but before we parted, I got him to fend to the *Commiffioners of Truft* then fitting at *Laghreagh*, for his Commiffion, and declared he would take upon him the Government. Whereupon to lofe no time, I gave him the beft account I could of the Forces in the Kingdom as well friends as foes: for he, during the War had been no more than a Spectator, beloved and refpected of all, and might have fo continued, had not his great Loyalty drawn him to take up this Commiffion (which was little lefs than to Sacrifice himfelf, and his) only to give the King time to try his Fortune

L with

with *Cromwell*, whose Armies were then near *Sterling* in *Scotland*, Encamped not far asunder, as the Kings Letters, brought by *Dean King* to us imported. We agreed at this meeting, that his Lordship should immediately raise 1000 Horse as an addition to the standing Forces in *Connaught*, and that I should March with my 1000 Horse out of the County of *Clare*, by *Limrick* to the Silver Mines, in the County of *Tipperary*, and be at such a day at the Rendezvouz, where I should meet with 1500 Foot he would send me, and a good officer.

I complyed punctually with my Orders, and the Mayor of *Limrick* as I Marched through the City on demand gave me 100 Foot. The Alarm of my March was soon known to Sir *Hardress Waller*, my Lord *Broghill* or both, lying near *Killmallock* with great Forces. They pursued me in all hast, and I Marched on to our appointed Rendezvouz, but could hear no news there, of the 1500

1500 Foot I was promised. Having lost this Anchor, I was put to my shifts, the Enemies coming on I had no other way but to thrust my self into the next fastness, and save my self as well as I could; but there was a Castle of the *OMaghers* that stood in the way, possess'd by the Enemy, and there being no other passage, I sent to the adjacent Villages, and got together Croes of Iron, Pickaxes, and what else could be found necessary, and fell a Storming of the Castle, and in three or four hours took it. In this place I kept the 100 men I had from *Limrick*, to secure the Pass, and being now pretty safe, I lodged that night at my ease: here Coll. *Fitz Patrick* came to me, who had for some time kept in those fastnesses, with a good Party of Foot and some Horse. My men being well refreshed, I took the plain Country near *Burras*, and after entring the Woods at the Foot of the Mountain *Sleave-Bleauma*, I met Sir *Walter Dungan* then Commissary General of the Horse, as was ordered. He brought with him only 300 Horse, and I finding my self still pursued with Horse and Foot, besides what were gathering round from all sides, I ordered Sir *Walter* to return from whence he came, and to stop all the Forces I had sent for, as well from *Ulster* as *Leinster*; thence with my 1000 Horse I Marched into *Connaught* passing by the Bridge of *Athloane*, and posted to *Loghreagh*, where my Lord Deputy then was, with a General Assembly sitting in his House. At my coming into his Chamber, I found about a dozen principal men of the Assembly, deputed to him, setting forth the desperate condition of the Nation, with the impossibility much further to hold out. Besides that there were now come to the Town, Mr. *John Grace*, and Mr. *John Bryan*, Commissioners from the Parliament or their Commander in Chief, offering greater Conditions than was reasonably to be expected as the Case stood. Whilst this Address was making,

making, my Lord was glad to see me come in, and ordered them to repeat what they had said. I seemed much Scandalized at the ill timing of their proposals, and therefore declared my dislike to them. Then by my Lords permission, (weary and dirty as I was) I went down into the Assembly being a Member, as a Peer of the Kingdom, and express'd my detestation of what they had in hand, demonstrating that if the 1500 men, commanded by Coll. *Burke* had not failed to meet me, as they promised at the Rendezvouz, I had probably now been Master of the Field; besides that the noise of a Treaty would destroy all that could be hoped for, from the endeavors against *Cromwell.* That his Majesty (as his own Letter signified) both to my Lord Deputy, and my self, made no doubt, if he could gain forty eight hours March towards *England* before *Cromwell*, but his business was done; because all were ready to joyn in his assistance; and therefore conjured us not to hearken to any Treaty with the Enemy. Then I set forth the State of the Forces of the Kingdom on all sides, and concluded very severely against the two *Parliament Commissioners*; so that they hastily packed out of Town, and the Assembly let the matter fall.

Reynolds now Besieged *Tehcrahan* in *Meath*, and my Lord Deputy came to *Tirrells* Pass about eight miles from it, with 2000 Foot, and 700 Horse; where a Council of War being held, I proposed that our Horse should Alarm the Enemy, whilst the Foot attempted through the Boggs to succour the Place; 'twas by all alledged impossible to be done, for coming near the place, there were two necks of Land, that did almost meet, and between them there was a great way or *Tougher*, with a large ditch of water on each side, which must be crossed, and that in all likelihood the Enemy would plant their Guns at both ends of this *Tougher*, and bring the strength of their Army to defend that Passage, there being no other way;

way; seeing we had no force to attack them on firm Land. I heard all this, and knew it very well, yet did not agree to the impossibility of entring the place; and therefore addressing my self to my Lord Deputy, I begg'd Pardon if I guessed at the thoughts of the Officers there present; which was, that I being General of the Horse, might well advance this undertaking, for I was to be with the Horse, and so to have no share in the Danger. But to shew the contrary, I desired his Excellency to give me the Command of that Party of Foot, and would venture to relieve the Town, through the Bogg, while the Horse Alarm'd the Enemy on the other side. It being thus determined, I entred the Bogg, which was eight miles long, with my two thousand Foot, and his Excellency took his March with the Horse, as was agreed. Coming in sight of this *Tougher*, I found the Enemy expecting, as we had supposed: for they saw me Marching from my first entring into the Bogg.

Then

Then I put my men into the best Order I could, in three Divisions, two to attempt passing the *Tougher*, the third Commanded by one Captain *Fox*, to stand still, and face two or three Battalions, that were drawn on my right hand, fearing they would fall on my Flank or Rear. Then I marched on with my two Divisions towards the *Tougher*, but coming within Shot, they raked me with their Cannon, and great Volleys of small shot. Nevertheless, I advanced still, and my men fought it on the *Tougher*, with handy-blows, and these that defended it retired to their Horse, which stood drawn up at each end of the *Tougher* on firm Land. Seeing this going so well I looked back and saw my third Division, (which was to stand still) coming after me. I ran to it crying to the Officer that Commanded to attack the Battalions, which he was ordered to look after. On this, he turn'd to his men, and spake something in *Irish*, that I did not know, and marched two or three hundred

dred paces in such a fashion, that I could not tell whether he intended fighting or running away. At last he did run away and all his Party followed, which when the two Divisions that had passed the *Tougher* saw, they marched on into the place, and I was left alone, only some Gentlemen with me, and by the favor of the night, (for now it began to be dark) I got off, and by the next morning returned to *Tyrrells* Pass. My Lord Deputy had all the story before my coming, and got the Captain secured that had caused this Disorder who being Tryed by a Council of War was Condemned, and shot to Death.

After this, *Ireton* knowing our Weakness two well, and that we did only keep a Bustle, till the King and *Cromwell* had decided their Quarrel, he again sate down before *Limrick*, with a powerful Army, on the County of *Limrick* side. I marched with what Forces could be drawn together, encamped at *Killaloo*, to observe

serve his Motions. He kept a Guard on his side of the River, as I did against him at *Bryans-Bridge*. and *Castle-Connell*. We lay in this manner a long time, he attempting nothing on the Town, or River, which was not Fordable in any place.

My Lord Deputy was at this time at *Gallway*, and writ to me in all hast to come to him. On my arrival, he told me, that the Abbot of St. *Katharine* was in the Harbor, and in his company many Officers, with a quantity of Arms, Ammunition, and other materials for War; that they were sent by the Duke of *Lorain* who pretended by some Agreement to be Protector Royal of the Kingdom of *Ireland* with power over all our Forces and Places, and to continue that Title and Dominion till after the War ended, he was reimbursed all his Expenses, and his Damages satisfied. I was much startled at the News; for though I strugled to keep up a Bustle, yet I never intended to buy it so dear as to give any footing or the least pretence

tence or title to any Foreign Prince. And having heard out his Lordship, I took the boldness to ask him, how far he was concerned in this matter. He protested before God, and upon his Honor he never gave Commission for any such Treaty; and as to the thing he knew no more than what he had told me, other than that the *General Assembly* then sitting in Town were in great Joy for this Succour, and pressed him earnestly for the Reception; but I found him intirely against it.

Being thus satisfied, I desired him to leave the matter to me, and let me deal with the Assembly. I went therefore immediately and found them on the debate, to which I spoke in my time; and with much detestation of the thing, declared all Traitors that were on such terms for receiving this Succour, and that I would hear no more of it, but return to my Forces, knowing what I had to do. My Lord Deputy was much pleased with this round discourse, and publickly approved

proved it: So the Abbot, with what he had, set Sail, and returned from whence he came.

At my return, (which was without delay) to *Killalow* I found all quiet, and whether *Ireton* had information of this passage I know not, but by a Trumpet I received from him a long Letter, four sides of Paper close written in a small hand; the drift was to set forth the justness of the Parliaments proceedings, their great power, how short a time I could subsist, what ill company I was with, and threw what dirt he could on the King I served; but concluded with great value of my Person, pitying my condition, and offering if I would retire and live in *England*, I should not only enjoy my Estate, but remain in safety with esteem and favor of the Parliament. This Letter I shewed immediately to Father *Peter Walsh*, whom I had always found faithful to the King and a great Lover of his Country. By his advice, and by the same Trumpet I answered all
his

his points, and rejected his propofition as to every particular, defiring him withal to fend no more Trumpets with fuch Errands. From this time there was an end of all Meffages and Letters between us.

All this while *Ireton* remained ftill and quiet, without any Action or Attempt, expecting the coming of Sir *Charles Coot* on my back or the fall of the River; both came together, and befides that, a third unlucky accident; for now fome days I kept Guards towards *Connaught*, when *Ireton* by Treachery of the Officer, one Captain *Kelly*, made himfelf Mafter of a Pafs called *Bryans Bridge*; whilft I was haftning with fome Troops to oppofe, having left the defence of the Pafs at *Killaloo* to Coll. *Fennel*, he Cowardly, or Treacheroufly quitted it, and with his Party fled into *Limrick*; where upon the Rendition of the Town, which was not long after, *Ireton*, with more than his ordinary Juftice, hanged him. Some fay he was carried to *Corke*, and there

there pleaded for his defence, not only this service, but how he had betrayed me before *Youghall*; but his Judges would not hear him on his Merits, but bid him clear himself of the Murthers laid to his Charge.

Now having Letters from my Lord Deputy, of Sir *Charles Coot*'s approach, I hastned to him with what Troops I had left, *viz.* about 300 Horse, and found him drawn into *Loghreagh* with his Forces; not being able to keep the Field against *Coot*, who was twice his number, yet did not think fit to attack him, and was gone by, before my coming. About this time, *Athlone* gave up to the Enemy, and so did *Limrick* to *Ireton* some weeks after. In the mean time, my Lord Deputy, and my self, with what Troops we had, retired towards *Jer-Connaught*, under the covert of the River, that runs by *Gallway*, and so shifted up and down, till Sir *Charles Coot* came before it on *Loghreaghs* side and had taken a Castle a little above

above on the River. Then we retired into *Gallway*, where we had not been long before we heard of the Kings Defeat at *Worcester*.

A man now would think this noble Lord had discharged his part; yet his zeal carried him farther: for he dispatched me for *France*, to the King by the way of *Innish-bofin*, (for the River of *Gallway* was full of Parliament Ships) with orders to set out the ill State of his Majesties affairs in *Ireland*; how the Enemy carried all before them; yet nevertheless to serve his Majesty, he intended after *Gallway* should be lost, to make a Mountain War and to give the Rebels trouble for some time, if his Majesty would but send him some small Succour, which he demanded, & appointed me to return with to *Innish-bofin*; a fit place for a Magazine, it being a large Island lying off *Jer-Connaught*, three miles into the Sea, in which we had a strong Garison. 'Tis surrounded with Rocks, and has but one entrance, where there is a pretty good
Har-

Harbour for Frigats and small Men of War. Here I shipped my self and Landed at *Brest*, ordering the Frigat that brought me, Commanded by Captain *Antonio Vandersip*, of *Bruges*, to expect my Orders. We had a sharp fight at Sea, with an *English* Ship, but foul weather parted us, and no great hurt was done, but the Bishop of *Down* kill'd in the Cabbin, 'tis thought, by the wind of a Bullet, or fear; for he had not the least sign of any hurt, and lived near a quarter of an hour.

Being Landed, I took post for St. *Germans*, where I found the King, Queen Mother, and my Lord of *Ormond*. I delivered my Letters of Credence, and in a day or two, had my Audience. They seemed to take it to heart, and consulted Cardinal *Mazarine*, and the chief Ministers. But the truth is, the King of *France*'s affairs were at that time so much in disorder, by reason of the Civil War, that nothing could be done. With this answer, the King gave me a Letter

ter to my Lord Deputy, acknowledging his good services and ordering he should make the best Conditions for himself and Party that he could, and expect a better season.

Wherefore having thus discharged my Commission, and seeing no hopes of success in *Ireland*, I discharged my Frigat, and with the Kings permission, engaged my self in the Service of the Prince of *Conde*, who was then joined with the *Spaniard*. But first I sent by a safe hand his Majesties Letter to my good Lord *Clanrickard*; of whom I have said so much already, that I need add nothing but my own esteem for his worthy memory, as a pattern of Loyalty. Between my leaving him and his laying down Arms, I can give no account of his Adventures, but have heard that he was driven to great Extremity.

AN APPENDIX.

IN the year 1638. being at *Rome*, I received a Letter from the late King *Charles* the Firſt, requiring me to attend him in his Expedition againſt the *Scots*, then Revolted and in Arms. Two days after I took poſt for *England*, and near *Turin* fell into an Army Commanded by the Marqueſs de *Leganes*, Governor of *Millan* for the King of *Spain*, who was Marching to joyn an other Army, then Beſieging that Place. But ſoon the Siege was raiſed, and I went into the Town where I found her Royal Highneſs the Dutcheſs of *Savoy* in great diſorder, as if ſhe had got no reſt in many nights. I taking leave of her, she gave me a Musquet Bullet, much battered, to deliver to her Sister the Queen of *England*, that came in at her Window, and missed her narrowly.

Arriving at *London*, I followed the King to *Berwick*; whom I found Encamped with a good Army near it, the River of *Tweed* before him; for the number, to this hour I never saw a better, and as I was told and believe, it could not be less than 16 or 17000 Horse and Foot, with a good Train of Arillery. Soon after my arrival there was a pacification; the next day I dined with *Lesly* General of the *Scots*, he shewed me his Army in Battalia, in number about 10 or 12000 Horse and Foot, but as to the Horses and Arms the twentieth man could not have passed Muster amongst any Armies I have since seen.

After this I passed my time as well as I could at home, till in the year 1640 the King of *France* Besieged *Arras*. On the news I went for *Bruxells*, and thence followed the Prince

Prince *Cardinal* (Governor of the *Low Countries*) to *Doway*, his Army intrenched near the Town, expecting the coming up of others, especially the Troops of the Emperor Commanded by *Lamboy*, and those of *Lorain*, by the Duke of *Lorain* himself. All being arrived, the whole Army marched, and coming to *Monte St. Aloy*, near the Enemies Line, Encamped on the Right by it; Many great Parties were sent out for the entring of Convoys, but they came so strong that little good was done upon them. The King of *France* being at *Amiens*, took care of all, whilst Mounsieur *Millerie, grand Master de L. Artillery*, press'd the Siege. Much time was trifled in this manner by the *Spaniards*; at length they attacked the Line, but were beaten off. Then Jealousies and Discontents began amongst the great ones, which daily increased, and the Arrearband beaten, where their Lieutenant General, the Count de *Bossue* was killed. The hopes of raising the Siege grew

Desperate, and at length the Town was rendred to the *French* (*Owen Roe ONeale*, afterwards General of the Province of *Ulster* for the Confederate Catholicks in *Ireland*, Commanded within.) The blame of not Succouring this place was laid on *Don Philip de Silva* General of the Horse under the Prince Cardinal. He was afterwards made Prisoner in *Spain* on Suspicion, as having betrayed the undertaking; but was after released, laying the fault on the first Minister then Governing that Monarchy under King *Philip* IV. as having done all by his orders, being the *Conde Duke*.

Having seen this Action I returned for *England* and sate in Parliament till the cutting off of the Earl of *Strafford*, and then I went for *Ireland*, where I had some Estate. And whilst I was there, broke forth the Rebellion of 1641. which kept me in War and Trouble till the Peace of 1646. as hath been seen. Then I went for *France*.

Coming

Coming to *Paris*, and hearing that *Landrise* was Besieged by the Arch-Duke *Leopoldus*, Governor of the *Low Countreys*, and that a *French* Army was gone to the Succour, I had the curiosity to see that Action. So I bought Horses and followed. Being come to the Army, in two or three days after we imbattelled before the Line, and so near, that the Enemies Cannon killed many men and horses in our Lines. I was in the first Line, a right-hand man in Prince *Ruperts* Troop, Commanded by Captain *Somerset Fox*, the Prince serving as Lieutenant General. Now it beginning to be dark, all were fitted for attacking the Line; and just as we expected the word to advance and fall on, we had orders to retreat in the silentest manner possible without the least touch of Drum or Trumpet. However the Enemy discovering it, came out, and did us some mischief in the Rear, and would have done more, if Prince *Rupert* that Commanded them, had not acted his part well.

By what I could hear as cause of this sudden change, the two Marshals, *Gastion* and *Ranso*, that Commanded, could not agree on the work they had in hand.

I returned from *Paris*, and remainned there, attending the *Queen* and Prince of *Wales* Orders (who were at St. *Germains*) till the year 1648. then I went for *Ireland* with the Marquess of *Ormond*, Lord Lieutenant, Serving the King against the *Nuncio, Council,* and other his Majesties Enemies, till 1651. after the Battel of *Worcester* lost, and *Cromwell* Conqueror of the three Kingdoms, and the King fled into *France,* whither I followed, and with his Majesties leave, engaged in the Prince of *Conde*'s Service (then joyned with the *Spaniards*) first, for a Troop of *Gens d' Arms*; soon after for a Regiment of Horse; but neither were ever mounted tho I had the men ready in *Paris,* as was ordered. Whilst I was thus, I came soon enough to the Rampart to see some part of the Fight in the Suburbs

burbs of St. *Anthony*, which began early in the morning *July* 2. 1652. The King of *France* looking on from the Hill of *Saronne*. The Prince of *Conde* hardly had time to Baracado the Avenues where he was attacked by *Monſieur de Jurain* commanding the Kings Army, with a Force much greater than his; the Fight was very bloudy, and had been fatal to the *Confederates*, had not the activity, beſides the Valor and Conduct of this brave Prince prevented it by riding from *Barrier* to *Barrier*, where his men were moſt preſſed; thus he entertained the Fight till about noon, that by means of *Madamoiſſelle d' Orleans*, the Gate of St. *Anthony* was opened for their Retreat into the City. After this the Confederates had all freedom in *Paris* till about the twelfth of *October* 1652. The Prince of *Conde*, Duke of *Lorain*, and the reſt of the Confederates left *Paris* and that night came to their Army at *Dammartin*, and took their March towards *Laſeite*, *Moline*, and *Fines*. I marched

marched with them, tho as a single man.

The first Place the Prince of *Conde* took (these Troops joyned) was *Ratele*, which he Besieged *Octob.* 27. 1652. took the out-works the twenty eighth, the Town the twenty ninth, and the Castle *Novemb.* 2. The Governor Monsieur *Rale*, *Chasteau Porsine* was Besieged at the same time, Yielded *Octob.* 28. making little resistance; then St. *Menehout* was Invested, the Prince of *Conde* and Duke of *Lorain* Commanding, and Rendred *November* 13. 1652. St. *Maurs* Commander. This place cost dear both in men and time by the mistake of the true attack, which discovered, and the Batteries changed, did not resist 12 hours.

About this time the Duke of *Orlean*'s Troops left us, the Duke having made his Peace.

November 23. 1652. the Prince took *Barleduke* after some days Siege, and a Breach made, Monsf. de *Fouge* Leiut. General of the *Lorain* Army was

was there killed with a Musquet-shot, viewing the Breach. *Comercy* Castle and Town about the same time was Surrendred to the Prince without much trouble.

The Castle of *Voyd* after some days Siege was Yielded *December* 9. to the Prince.

Now the Marshal *de Turenne* having gotten a good Army together, came near us, and Besieged *Barleduke*, which in a few days he regained; and whilst this was doing Surprized the Town of *Comercy*, where my self with many others were taken Prisoners; but the Count *de Fiesque*, who Commanded, being in the Castle maintained it. Monsieur *Marole* Governor of *Tunvile* who did this Feat, the next day brought me to the Quarters of Monsieur *de la Ferte*, who gave me leave on my Parole to visit the Duke of *Yorke* in the Quarter of Monsieur *de Turenne*. His Royal Highness at my Request got me to be exchanged, so I returned to the Prince, and the Officer exchanged went to the

the Marshal *de la Ferte*, of whose Army he was, this Campaigne ended with our having taken *Uernience* after a Breach made which was the twenty ninth of *January* 1652.

April 23. 1653. The Prince of *Conde* arrived in *Bruxels*, and was Lodged in the Palace. The Campaigne following *Septem.* 5. 1653. We Besieged *Roeroy*, the Seventh the Line of Circumvallation was begun, and finished the twelfth; the Trenches opened the eleventh; the *Spaniards*, *Italians*, and *Germans* had each an attack; the twenty second the three Nations were lodged on the Counterscarp. Sharp Sallies were made, with some loss to the Besiegers; however they held their ground, and fastned a Miner to one of the Bastions which Mine was ready to spring the twenty sixth. The next night the Mine was sprung, and a Breach made in the face of the Bastion, something too near the point; however our People lodged themselves, and the Enemy retrenched in the Bastion; but not being able to

make

make it good, the Garison much weakned with the loss of men killed and hurt, *October* 1. 1653. the place was rendred. I never knew Bombs annoy any place so much as this. From the first day of this Siege to the last, nothing but Rain, with ill weather; and that which was worse; the Prince of *Conde* desperately sick all the time: However tho he lay in his bed, nothing of consequence was done but by his advice; tho the *Arch-Duke Leopoldus* Commanded in Chief: the Governor of the place was the Chevalier *Montague*, who as I remember was brought out wounded: The Duke of *Lorain*'s Troops, Commanded by the Count of *Luniville*, assisted in this Siege; at which the Duke seemed to be ill pleased, for he was angry with *Luniville*, and rebuked him severely.

February 26. 1654. The Duke of *Lorain* being in *Bruxels*, and his Army near the Town, was arrested by the Count *de Garrisie*, Master de Gamp General, so ordered by the Arch-Duke

Duke *Leopoldus*, and conveyed to the Castle of *Antwerp*: But prince *Francoys* of *Lorain*, being at *Vienna*, was sent for, which appeased the Officers, especially when he arrived at *Bruxels*, which was the ninth of *May* following. All this time, besides the quality of Marshal de Camp, I had the particular Command of nine or ten Regiments of *Irish*, making 5000 men; and the Campaign coming on, the Prince ordered me to make a detachment of 1000 of the choicest men I had dividing them into Fifties, Commanded by Lieutenants; only one Fifty might have a Captain, and then to deliver them to the Count de *Briole*, Marshal de Camp, which I did, tho with much murmur of the Colonels, and other Officers, concluding never to see their men again, which fell out true, being to be sent as far off as to *Clermont, Stevy,* and other places.

Next Campaign began with the King of *France*'s Besieging *Steny* which he did *June* 9. 1654. The

Spani-

Spaniards thought to raise his Siege by attacking another place, and Besieged *Arras*, investing it the third of *July* 1654. Monsieur *Moudieux* Governor; the Lines of Circumvallation finished the ninth, not so large by two Leagues as when the *French* took it; the twelfth or thirteenth the Trenches were opened; tho the Chevalier *de Crequi* with some hundreds of Horse had entred the Town. The sixth or seventh of *July* some other attempts were made to put in Succour, but none hit to any purpose. It is certain our Army was no way provided or sufficient for the work, to Man so large a Line, and furnish the attacks; which were two; one the *Spaniards*, the other the Prince of *Conde's*. The *Lorainers* Commanded by Prince *Francoys* had no attack. The ground was such that the Ditch of the Line in most places could hardly be made of any depth; to supply which defects eight or ten roes of great holes were made before it, with Stakes like Pallisads beaten into them.

Whilst

Whilst we were now carrying on our attacks, with much art and Valour, Monsieur *de Turenne* with a small Army Posted himself at *Montriporeux*, and *Vittry* about a League from our Line, almost in the way to *Doway*; from whence much of our Provisions and other things came. But when *Steny* was Yielded, being *August* 6. the Count *de Camillie* Governor and the Marquess *de Fabert* Commanding the Army that took it; the King with this Army Marched and Posted himself near Mount S. *Aloye*, not far from our Line, so that in truth we were in a manner now Besieged, but quickly put out of our pain. For soon after being the 24*th*. or 25*th*. of *August*, an hour before day our Line was Alarm'd round, attacked really in two or three places, and forced in a short time. Thus *Arras* was relieved, and our Army retreated to *Cambray*. After this *Quency* yielded to the *French*, so this Field ended. I do not remember any thing remarkable that passed in the year 1655. but the 15*th*. of *June* 1656.

1656. Mounsieur *de Turenne* invested *Valencennes*; to the Succour of which *Don John* Governor of the *Low-Countrys*, having gotten his Army together Marched; the Prince of *Conde* with his Army joyned, they posted themselves the first of *July* at *Farmars*, a League from the Town, (and very near the Enemies Line) where they Intrenched. *June* 28. the *French* opened their Trenches with two attacks from the two Armies, of *Turenne* and *la Ferte*. Much scuffling there was at this Siege between the Town and the Enemy, many brave Sallies were made and as gallantly opposed, several Works taken by the *French*, and regained by the Garison. The Governor, the Duke *de Burnaville* caused Sluces to be opened, which raised waters in the Enemies Camp, and much hindred the Communication between the two Amies of *Lorain* and *la Ferte*; till one morning before day, being *July* 16. *Don John* and the Prince of *Conde* fell on the Enemies Line, Alarming it on all

all sides, and where they attacked it really entred, tho it cost much blood on both sides, many Prisoners were taken of the *French*, one of which was the Marshal *de la Ferte*; *Valencienne* thus relieved.

July 21. 1656. The *Spaniards* and Prince of *Conde* Invested *Conde*, Monsieur *de Paſſage* Governor; *August* 8. they finished their Line of Circumvallation, and the place being vigorously attacked, was Rendered *Aug.* 17. Here ended this Campaigne.

The next Field was begun by the same Prince and Army, besieging St. *Gilaine March* 16. 1652. Monsieur *de Chomburge* Governor; the Story is not worthy to be remembred for the place was betrayed by some of the Garison, and so Rendered *March* 22. Soon after, being *May* 20. 1657. The Marshal *de Turenne* Invested *Cambray*, and took his Posts for the Siege, but the Prince of *Conde* being at *Boseu*, near *Monts*, marched immediately with 4000 Horse, and the 29*th*. in the Evening came near the

the Enemys Camp; the next morning an hour before day fell on Monsieur *de Turenne*'s Quarters, broke through into the Town and relieved it: However, the *French* lost no Courage, but the 26*th.* of *August* following Besieged S. *Venant*, and about the same time *Don John*, the Duke of *York*, and Prince of *Conde* Besieged *Ardares*; and for the better dispatch, the 28*th.* they made a general Assault, taking all the outworks and fastned Mines to the Walls in three places. But St. *Venant* yielding sooner than was expected, the Princes were forced to raise their Siege.

Mardike was Besieged by the *French, September* 29. 1657. and taken in five days.

The next Campaign began *May* 14. 1658. When the Marshal *d' Aumont*, attempting to gain *Lestend* by Intelligence and Surprisal, was taken himself in his own Net. The particular Relation is pleasant; but it having been often printed, I'll let it alone; now tho this Marshal of *France* fell into this misfortune, Monsieur *de Turenne* did abundantly recover the Honour. For the 24*th.* of *May* 1658. he Besieged *Dunkirk.* *Don John,* the Duke of *York,* and Prince of *Conde,* with all the Force they could make, came to the Succour, and it seems, with confidence that *Turenne* durst not appear without his Line, for otherwise they would not have come near so ill provided, most of their Horse being gone to Forrage, or scattered up and down, and their Cannon not arrived. But Monsieur *de Turenne* failed them; for knowing they came from *Furnes,* he marched to meet them. On the *Downs* thus they encountred the fourteenth of *June* 1658. and after much fighting the honour of the Field remained to the *French.* Yet the Town held stoutly tho the Succors were beaten; for it never Capitulated till the 14*th.* of *July,* that their brave Governor, the *Marquess de Lede* was wounded mortally, of which he died; so the Town yielded the same day.

The

The *French* being in this humor of Conquering, Monsieur *la Ferte* Besieged *Graveling* the 27th or 28th. of *July* 1658. it Capitulated the 28th. of *Aug.* and was Rendered the next day.

Soon after this the Prince *de Lione*, General of the Horse for the King of *Spain*, his Army being Routed near *Ipres*, he with part of his Horse saved themselves into the Town, on which the *French* Besieged them, and in 4 or 5 days the Town was yielded being *Septemb.* 24. the Prince and Garison as I think remaining Prisoners of War.

Octob. 27. 1658. The *French* took *Comines*, which made some resistance.

Now a suspension of Arms concluded *May* 9. 1659. being followed with the *Pyrenean* Peace Signed *Novemb.* 7. 1659. put an end to the War which had so long raged.

From this time there was no more War in this part of the World, till the King, after his Restauration, brake with the *Hollanders*, and much fighting there was at Sea; in some of which I have been, tho but a Voluntier.

tier. Thus, and following the Court I paſſed my time till the year 1667. that the *French* Invaded *Flanders*, the Marqueſs of *Caſtle-Roderigo* Governor. Thither by his Majeſties Command I went with 2400 men, a Recruit for the old *Engliſh* Regiment, of which I was made Colonel; and about *June* 15. 1667. with ſome of them Landed at *Oſtend*, the reſt ſoon following. Theſe men were immediately thrown into Towns, as *Newport, Lille, Courtrey, Audenard*, &c. But before my coming the King of *France* had ſeized *Armentiers, Charleroy, Bergen,* St. *Winoke, Feurnes, Aeth*; and in four or five days after took *Tourney* which reſiſted three days. Till about this time the *Spaniards* did not know themſelves abſolutely to be in War; for their Troops often met the *French*, and parted as Friends. Then Monſieur *de Turenne* Beſieged *Doway July* 1. had it the 6th.

July 18. 1667. *Courtrey*, with the Citadel was taken by the *French*, having made ſome reſiſtance, but *Audenard ward* at the same time made little or none.

Aug. 5. The King of *France* having for some days attempted the taking of *Desmond*, left it after the loss of many men, as reported: But the King soon after Besieged *Lile*, opened the Trenches before it *August* 19. It yielded the 27*th.* after most of the out-works taken; the Count *de Broy* Governor.

Now the Count *de Marcine*, Maister de Camp General for the King of *Spain*, was at this time in *Ipres* with a considerable Body of Horse, and some Foot, of which I had 6 or 700 of my Regiment, he pretending to Succour *Lile*. But on the news of its Rendition he marched away with all his Horse, hoping to Recover *Gaunt*, but whether by reason of the ill ways and foul weather or other hindrances, came short; for the *French* Horse and Dragoons were gotten before him, and Encamped near *Mary-kirk*, not far from the Town, on *Hollands* side of the cut River that goes between *Gaunt* and

and *Bruges*; and the last of *August* early in the morning) having no right Intelligence of the Enemy) fell in amongst the *French* Horse. Thus surprised and marching on Dikes, he was enforced to fight for it, and as men catched, in this manner, after some dispute, was Routed, many of his Men and Officers killed and taken prisoners, himself narrowly escaping. The *French* thus encouraged fell on *Aloft*, midway between *Bruxels* and *Gaunt*, and being assaulted, it was Rendered *Septemb.* 9. or 10. 1667.

Now to save what was left of the *Low-Countries*, there was no other Remedy, (for Army we had none) but by the mediation of the Neighbour Princes to gain a suspension of Arms, published *March* 6. 1668. and was to hold till the last of the Month; then there was a second Suspension of Arms, which began the 15*th*. of *April* following, and was to last to the end of *May*. But he Peace of *Aix la Chapell* concluded on *May* 2. following, put an end to our trouble: for it cannot be called a War. After

After this the Marquefs of *Castle-Roderigo* staid not long; but the Conftable of *Castile* succeeded, in whofe time all was quiet.

Since the peace of *Aix*, the *Spanish Netherlands* enjoyed a shew of quietnefs, till about *Octob*. 4. 1673. Then at a meeting between the Count *de Monterey*, Governor of the *Low-Countries*, and the Prince of *Orange*, at a Village near *Antwerp*, called *Galmethat*, within half a League of the Priory of *Huybergnen*, *Spain* was engaged in a new War againft the *French*, both Parties feeming inclined to a Breach.

I do not know all the reafons, but for a long time each complained of Infractions: The *French*, that the *Spaniards* had affifted the Prince of *Orange* in his attempt for the Surprize of *Charleroy*, in which he failed, fent of their Troops to Man certain Towns belonging to the States of *Holland*, as *Bolduke*, *Berginopsome*, and other places; that their Troops were affifting the Prince of *Orange*, in the taking

king of *Narden* near *Amsterdam*, &c.

The *Spaniards* complained that the Kings Countries were eaten up and destroyed by the marching of *French* Troops through them, especially when the King of *France* with his Army entred about *Bruges* and *Gaunt*, Marching at discretion, fearing no Enemy till he came to *Bruxels*, where he Encamped on all sides several days. After this refreshment he continued his March to *Maestricht*, which he Besieged *June* 11. 1673. and took it the 30*th*. That the Prince of *Conde* had for several weeks lain with an Army, eating and destroying the Country of *Alost*.

Now on the breaking out of this new War, the Marshal *de Belford*, who Commanded for the King of *France* in *Holland*, had order to draw all his Forces thence, and March to *Maestricht*.

This alarm'd the Count *de Montery*, fearing that he would take *Ruremond* in his way. So he sent me to Command there, being General *de Battle*.

But

But the Marshall spared me, and picked up *Erklanes*, a small Town two Leagues from me seated on the *Rore*; being passed, he joyned the Prince of *Conde* near *Maestricht*, and alarm'd *Stevenswert*, a regular place and tenable, when there is no want within it; I in an hours time received two Orders from the Count *de Montery*, brought by two reform'd Officers, sent express, requiring me on sight to march with the Count of *Mansfield* and 500 of the *Germans*, in Garison with me, and to endeavour the getting into *Stevenswert*, where I was to Command, and if I were worsted in the Attempt, to save my self, and such as remained after the fight to *Venlow*. I received these Orders as I was at Dinner, about one of the Clock, and got into the place with my men by six of the Clock that Evening, tho it were three or four Leagues, for the place was not Invested, as the Count *de Montery* thought; however, these Armies kept us in doubt four or five days, till at length the Prince of *Conde* having taken

taken the Castle of *Argento*, they Besieged *Newliny, May* 20. 1674. a Fort belonging to the King of *Spain*, on the River *Meux*, Seated between *Liege* and *Maestricht*. It was Rendered *May* 23. After this the Prince of *Conde* having trifled some time in Marching up and down came with his Army to *Pieton*, a strong Post in its nature by reason the meeting of the two Rivers of *Samber* and *Pieton*; but withal he was strongly intrenched, and had much Cannon on his Batteries, and Cavaliers.

About the 15*th*. of *July* 1674. *Dinant* with the Castle was Surprized by the Imperialists, Commanded by the Count *de Souch*; and *July* 22. following they passed the *Meux* near *Namurs* to joyn the Prince of *Orange*, and other the Confederates. Now all being together, after several Campings they came to *Nivell*, hoping to draw the Prince of *Conde* from his Entrenchments to a fair Battel, shewing themselves in Battel before him. Several days passed thus. Then they march'd from *Nivell Aug*. 9.

and

and the next day Encamped at *Seneff*, *Jelny*, and other places thereabouts. All this while the Enemy never appeared, tho by coming near many occasions were offered. Seeing nothing could prevail, *Aug.* 11. 1674 the Prince of *Orange*, with the Confederates, very early in the Morning marched off, intending to Encamp between *Marymont* and *Binch*. But being to pass within a little League of the Enemys Camp, they made a detachment of 5000 Horse and Dragoons, for the better Security of the Rear. In the March the *Imperialists* had the Van-guard, the *Hollanders* the Battel, the *Spaniards* consisting of sixteen Squadrons of Horse; The Rear-guard now having marched some time in this Manner, about ten or eleven of the Clock in the Morning, being *Saturday*, the Enemy began to appear, attacking the River, and though well disputed, carried all before them for some hours, till the *Germans* turned, and joyned with some of the *Holland* Army not broken, gave a stop

stop to this furious beginning, and brought it to a bloudy Battel. Both sides bragged of Victory, tho neither had much cause. The Fight ended *Sunday* morning, and that night the Confederates Encamped where they were to have been the night before. And the Prince of *Conde* returned to his Retrenchment at *Pieton*.

The Prince of *Orange* being a Stranger and having left himself and Army to be guided by a General that pretended to know the Country, was brought so near the Prince of *Conde*'s retrenchment, that in going off his Rear was exposed, and so accordingly it was attacked. But next day after the Battel, the Prince complained much, and fell very heavy on the General who advised this March; but it was too late.

These were the most powerful Armies that had been seen in *Flanders* these many years. I believe the Confederates did much pass in number, tho the Prince of *Conde*'s Army in most mens Judgments exceeded Forty ty thousand Horse and Foot. The report of the Slain and Wounded is various, but they may be taken at eight or ten thousand of both sides. I know not which lost most; but the quality exceeded the number. Amongst many other brave men were slain the Marquess *de Assentar*, Master de Camp General for the *Spaniards*, and Sir *Walter Vane* Major General; Serving the *Hollanders*.

The Prince of *Orange* after this Battel of *Seneff* lost no time, for *September* 17. following he had formally Besieged *Audenard* (the Sieur *de Rospaine* Governor) and having much advanced his Trenches, had notice of the Prince of *Conde*'s approach, with his Army increased, the Marshal *de Humers* having joyned to him 8 or 10000 men. On this the Confederates drew most of their men out of the Attacks, but remained within the Line until the next morning, and then with the favour of a dark mist quitted all, left the Siege, and got to *Gaunt*, I know not how, but

certainly

certainly in great confusion, after the loss of many men. Much blame was laid on the Count *de Souch*; whether he were faulty or no, he soon with his Army return'd for *Germany*, and the Prince of *Orange* posted for *Grave* (long Besieged by General *Ravenholt*, a *Holland* Commander) and took it about *October* 22. 1674. the Army of the States General left *Flanders*, and returned to their Country.

The King of *France* began his Campaign the year 1675. with the Siege of *Limburg*. The Prince of *Orange* and Duke of *Villa-Hermosa*, then Governor of the *Low Countrys*, assembled their Armies near *Louvain*, and Marched in all hast to its Succour, tho in miserable weather. They passed the *Meuse* at *Roermond*; but before they could arrive at the Enemies Camp, the place was yielded *June* 20. after a very good defence, the Prince of *Nassaw* Governor of it, and the Province.

The Appendix. 31

The Army of the Confederates much shattered, and in disorder with so terrible a March, being returned to *Aerscot* Encamped there, and near about for a long time, till being well refreshed and recovered, they began their March towards *Monts*; and *Binch*, without the Armies coming to it, yielded to a Party, sent by the Prince of *Orange, Aug.* 31. 1975.

The Campaign of the year 1676. began with the King of *France*'s Besieging *Conde*, which he did *April* 19. The Prince of *Orange*, the Duke *de Villa-hermosa*, Marched to its Succor, but coming near found it rendered, the 25*th.* of the same Month, not being able to resist longer the several Assaults the *French* made.

The King of *France* not contenting himself with *Conde*, sent his Brother the Duke of *Orleans*, and the Marshal *de Crequi* to Besiege *Bouchain*, which they did, *May* 5. 1676. and the King to cover the Siege Encamped at *Keverine* facing towards *Monts*; the River before him. On this Intelligence

ligence some days after, the Prince of *Orange* and Duke *de Villa-Hermosa*, being with their Army Encamped near *Mons*, Marched, and on Bridges of Boats, before day, passed *L'Escaulte*, within *Cannon* shot of *Conde*, leaving it on the left hand; and not losing time, about ten or eleven of the Clock that Morning, being *May* 9. gained the height between *Valenciennes* and the Abbey of *Bone Esperance*. But coming there, we found the King of *France* on a height Embattelling his Army before us, about half a League distant, all plain between the two Armies, and just in the way between us and *Bouchain*, so near we were, that the Cannon killed from one Army to the other. Thus posted, those that were not of the Great Council thought of nothing but immediately to fall on, and I my self was one of those; for it being my fortune that Campaigne to Command the King of *Spain's* Foot, I made many Speeches to them, preparing them to Battel, fitting them with Powder, and all things

things needful. But the day paſt, we lay by our Arms all night, and in the morning had orders to encamp, throwing up a Line before us, *Bouchain* (Monſieur *Drouhte* Governor) ſeeing this Succour did its part; but at laſt, being over-preſſed, the place yielded the 12*th*. or 13*th*. of *May*; yet the King, at the head of his Army, ſtood facing us five or ſix days more till *Bouchain* was put in Order, and all Lines and Trenches levelled. Then the 19*th*. of *May*, before day, after his Drums and Trumpets had done their parts, he Marched off from his Camp at the Farm of *Hurtisbe*, and that night Encamped near *Bouchain*; the next day march'd for *Doway*. Theſe were great Armies, each counted at leaſt 50000 men; but what ever they were I am aſſured they were not leſſned by ſo long lying near Neighbors.

After this the Prince of *Orange* Marched from his Camp of *Mon d' Anſin* near *Valencennes May* 21. and after ſeveral Campments came to *Nivelle*, from whence the 8*th*. of

July with a Detachment of his Army and some others that met him, the 11th. or 12th. of *July* he Invested *Maestricht*, the 19th. the Lines of Circumvallation were finished, and the 20th. he began to make use of his Cannon, opening his Trenches by two attacks, one was the Bishop Prince of *Osnaburg*'s; the other the Prince of *Orange*'s own; *Wick*, on the other side of the *Meuse* was not attacked. Now whilst this Siege was carrying on, the Duke *de Villa-hermosa* marched with the Army of *Holland* and his own the 26th. of *July* to *Marykirk* near *Gaunt*, and *Aire* having been Besieged for some days by the Marshal *de Humiers*, the Duke Marched to *Deinse*, where he heard that the Fort *Link* was taken, and soon after *Aire*. The cause given why this strong place held out no better is, that a Magazine of powder blew up by some accident; on which the Burgers (more strong than the Garison) seized the Governor, the Marquess *de Warny*, and compelled him to demand a Treaty.

This

This having broken the Duke's Measures, for he design'd to have ventured for the Succor of *Aire,* his Excellency Marched immediately, following the Count *de Waldike,* who was gone before him with the *Holland* Army, and Encamped between *Lovain* and *Bruxels,* his Excellence Encamped near *Mechlir*; but *Aug.* 20. he left his Camp, and in some days both the Armies came to *Tongres*; and soon after appeared the Van of the *French* Army, so that he had no more time than to call a Council of War, where having heard the relation, given by Count *de Waldike* newly come from the Siege, not being above two Leagues distance, unanimously all gave their opinions for the present raising the Siege, and that the Duke and *Waldike* should let the Prince know so much: accordingly the next day the Siege was raised, the Enemy putting in Succor.

 The Prince then drawing off, all our Enemies being joyned, were put in Battel on a height, about half a

League from the Line. But Monſieur *deSchomberg* having relieved the place marched another way, and Encamped that night on the Hill of St. *Peters*. I was in the Trenches before the Siege was raiſed; but did not judge the Town ſo preſs'd as was generally ſaid, without it had ſome want within, that I knew not; for there were many hard Pieces to be gained before Miners could be faſtned to the Wall, or any attackable breach made with Cannon. This was by much the bloodieſt Siege that ever I ſaw. The *Reingrave*, with a great part of the men that made the Princes Court, were killed, and more hurt; the Prince himſelf ſhot in the Arm; all the Regiments ſtrangely diminiſhed; the Cannon was loſt; for coming from *Holland* by the River of *Meux*, when it was pretty full, now it being much fallen, it could not be brought off. By what I ſaw of the Line of Circumvallation, I would rather have choſen to fight in a plain field than behind it; for it was not of ſtrength

ſuffici-

sufficient; neither was the Army of Force to Man it, and go on with their attacks, without the Prince had drawn into his Line the Army Commanded by the Duke *de Villa-hermosa* and *Waldike*. That possibly might have changed the Scene, tho the Communication would have been very hard, between them of *Wick*-side, with those before *Maestricht*, because of the River *Meuse*, which above and below must have been passed on Bridges of Boats: From the first of the Siege I never heard the Garison counted at less than five or six thousand men. I shall not venture to give a Judgment of the men killed and wounded; but certainly the number was great. The dividing the Army was in my opinion ill advised, neither party being of strength to do the work designed for it, whereas united it might have either carried *Maestricht*, or hindred the taking any other place. And for all the Princes exposing himself and Army to the uttermost of danger, yet some there were

were that did not afford him a good word, but the Contrary. After the raising this Siege the Prince of *Orange* fought by all means to engage the *French* in a Battel; yet about *Sep.* 7. 1675. Monsieur *Schomberge* passed the River of *Mahaine* in the view of our right wing uninterrupted, but the Prince was in the left Wing near a League distance, and hardly knew any thing till all was past. About three days after, the Prince and Duke *de Villa-Hermosa* Incamped the Army about *Giblow*, the quarter of the Court in the Town, and Monsieur *de Schomberge* with his Army, about a League from us, in a fast Country, but very great Plains just before him. The next morning early the Prince put his Army in Battel on this Plain, in sight and very near the Enemy, but *Schomberge* stirred not. Now after some hours, wearied with standing, the Prince with his Army marched off, leaving the *Spaniards* and *Germans* in the Rear; which soon after that began to move,

Monsieur

Monſieur *Montal*, with a great Body of Horſe and Dragoons marched through *Giblow*, from whence we parted, and fell on in the Flank and Rear, doing ſome miſchief, cauſing great confuſion among us. And had this Party been well ſeconded by Monſieur *Schomberge*, it might have proved a ſecond *Seneff*; for the Prince of *Orange* with his Army was far off, and many of his Horſes gone to Forrage. In a day or two after the Prince went for the *Hague*, and the Duke *de Villa-hermoſa* with *Waldike* Marched to *Wawer* in order to putting an end to the Field of 1676.

This year 1677. The Field opened with the Count *de Nancres* attacking the Fort, called the three holes near *Vilverde*, on the cut River that goes between *Bruxels* and *Antwerp*; but was beaten off the 24th. of *February*.

The 6th. or 7th. of *March*, *Valenciennes* was Beſieged by the King of *France*; he opened his Trenches the 9th. and the 17th. the Town was taken

taken by Surprise about nine of the Clock in the morning. The story is strange, for half an hour before this accident, and the 8th. day the Trenches opened the Enemy had not gained a foot of ground; the *French* entred by the Gates, which they found open, for the Governor, the Marquess of *Risburge*, a brave Soldier, was in his bed dangerously wounded, and the Town was Governed by a Council of War. Thus encouraged, the King Besieged *Cambray* about the last of *March* following, and the third or fourth of *April* the Town yielded; after the Garison, by orders of the Governor, had killed all their Horses, being as I have heard near 1000. then with the Governor they retired into the Cittadel, which was fiercely attacked; but the King having a mighty Force, divided his Army, and with one part his Brother, the Duke of *Orleans*, Besieged St. *Omers* March 28. 1677. On which the Prince of *Robeck*, Governor, sent pressing Letters to the Prince

Prince of *Orange* (then Encamped in the *Pais de Waft* near *Gaunt*) to haften to his Succor. The Prince of *Orange* on this, and his great zeal for the Service did what he could to put his Army in order, having none but his own with him; and the 11th. of *April,* after hard marching, coming to *Caftles,* found the Duke of *Orleans* had quitted the Line to meet him, and was in Battel before him. Then the two Armies engaged, and the Battel was well fought on both fides for a long time; but the detachment fent from *Cambray* by the King of *France* turned the Scales.

This, together with the Princes fighting on ground he knew not, and where he met with Rivers and Defiles or narrow ways that he never heard of, was the caufe of his overthrow.

Soon after this, *April* 17. the Citadel of *Cambray* was rendered, Don *Pedro de Saval* Governor of it and the Town: and St. *Omers* about the 28th. of *April* following was likewife rendered.

This

This did not abate the Courage of the Prince of *Orange*; for *Aug.* 4. following (almoſt in the view of as good an Army as that he Commanded) he Beſieged *Charleroy,* a place ſeated on the River *Sambre,* ſtrong by nature, and Fortified with all art imaginable, a Gariſon of four or five thouſand men, a brave Governor, the Count *de Montal,* no want within, but rather abundance of every thing; very hard to make a good Line of Circumvallation, for beſides the Rockineſs of the Ground, one part of it muſt be commanded by a hill, that could not be ſecured but by an Army without, near as ſtrong as any that might come for the Relief; a great wood that runs ſeveral Leagues in length, and in breadth near half a League, joyns to this Line; thro this there are great Ways or Lanes cut, where two or three Squadrons might march in Breaſt: but the Stumps and ſome fallen Trees remain ſtill, ſo that Horſe or Man could hardly paſs but in paths; the place not attackable

ble but on one side, and by reason of the *Sambre* that runs by it, which must be passed by Bridges of Boats, the communication very difficult. Thus the Prince lay Besieging this place, whilst the Duke *de Villa-hermosa* with an Army was encamped on the said Hill, till the Duke of *Luxemburgh* came with his Army, and encamped within little more than Cannon-shot of the Wood, in a great Plain, over against our Camp, I mean that Camp Commanded by the Duke *de Villa-hermosa*, who lay without the Line, for the defence of the mentioned Hill: On this Campment of the Duke of *Luxemburgh* many Councils of War were held by the great ones of the Confederates: The Duke *de Villa-hermosa*, and the *Spanish* Generals were for passing the Wood, and engaging the Enemy. But the Prince of *Orange* and his Generals judged it not feisable, and further, impossible to succeed with the work in hand, this powerful Army so near. Whereupon the Prince resolved to raise the Siege,

Siege, which he did in good order *Aug.* 14. 1678. The reason given by the Chief Confederate Generals for advising or consenting to this Siege of *Charleroy*, is, that for many days both Armies had been encamped near together in the Country of *Aloft*; but the *French* could not be brought to a Battel. Now the Confederates finding themselves very strong, fell on this design, hoping to gain their end in Besieging this important place, by the Enemies coming to its Succour. This might hold pretty well if the Confederates had pursued their point, when the *French* came as they could wish. For the Duke of *Luxemburgh* with his Army passed the *Sambre* at *La Busiere*, and so kept on his March till he came to the Encampment near the Wood, which took up at least two days; in all which time he could not well have avoided fighting, if the Confederates had sought it, by Marching to meet them. This failure is hard to be excused. Much blame was laid on the Prince of *Orange*

Orange for not paſſing the Wood, and attacking the *French* in their Camp, which if he had done, according to all reaſons of War, he had loſt his Army, for the *French* would never have given him time to have put his Army in Battel, but fought him by piece-meals as he appear'd out of the Wood. Beſides, his Battalions and Squadrons muſt needs have been diſordered in their March through the Wood. The Generals that were for Fighting, alledged that the *French*, by reaſon of a little River before them were ſo Encamped that their right Wing could not ſuccour their left. But ſuch an Encampment is hardly credible, it being in a great plain where they had choice of Encampment. It was further given out, and ſpoken publickly, that the Prince raiſed the Siege on ſome Letter or Meſſage the King of *England* ſent him, and brought by the Earl of *Oſſory*. Now, to my own knowledge, and to the view of all the Army, the Earl of *Oſſory* came to the Prince ſome days before *Charleroy*

was

was Invested, so that this Message or Letter might have prevented the Siege rather than to have raised it. Besides, if the King of *England*, moved by interest of State, should have sent such Letter or Message, is it to be imagined that he would have imployed the Earl of *Ossory*, who was one of the bravest men of his time, and, if he had a fault, too fond of Glory? Thus you see in what ill station the Prince of Orange was.

As we return'd from this Siege the 24th. of this Month, *Binch* fell into our hands, and in a day or two after we took *la Buthire*, but with some shot of Cannon.

Soon after this, *Septemb.* 10. the Duke of *Luxemburgh* attacked the Fort, called the *Three Holes*, near *Vilvoid*. The attack began about ten in the morning, and the night ended it; there were not in it above sixty men, Commanded by one Captain *Carpenter*; he and they got much honour, and the *French* went off with loss of some men.

The

The Appendix. 47

The Prince of *Orange* being in *England* or at the *Hague*, I know not whether, the Marshal *de Humiers* Besieged St. *Guilain*. The Duke *de Villa-hermosa*, now Commanding in chief, for Monsf. *Waldike*, with the *Holland* Army, was to obey his Orders, marched for its Succor; but coming in sight, found the place yielded, or treating, it being the 10th. or 11th. of *December*. The *French* resolving to give little rest, the King fell on *Gaunt* the 9th of *March* 1678. and had it the 18th. the Castle held out two days more. The reason that *Gaunt* made little Resistance, was, it had no Garison for so great a place; the Burgers did what was done.

The King from *Gaunt* marched to *Ipres*, it having been restored to the *Spaniards* upon the *Pyrenian* Peace, and Besieged it, opening the Trenches before both Town and Cittadel the 18th. and 19th. of *March* 1678. And as it had a brave Governor, the Marquess *de Conflant*, so it was well defended; but being vigorously attacked,

tacked, the Cittadel good for nothing, and many things wanting in the Town, *March* 27. it was yielded.

The *French* left no stone unturned for gaining of places. For a Party sent from *Maeſtricht* the 4th. of *May* 1678. in the night ſurprized *Leewe*, a very ſtrong and important place, not far from *Lovain*. Since the taking of St. *Guillian* by the *French*, *Monts* had been very cloſely blocked, and ſo much ſtreightned, that if not ſpeedily relieved, it muſt yield, having many wants within. On this the Prince of *Orange*, and Duke *de Villa-Hermoſa* reſolved to attempt its ſuccor: And having gotten a good Army together, marched, and arriving near *Soigne*, the Duke of *Luxemburgh* with his Army retired before them towards *Monts*; but coming within a League or thereabouts, Encamped himſelf on a large Heath, with the Valley of *Caſtio* before him, his back towards the Town. The Confederates coming near this Valley, and in full view of of the Enemies Camp, the Valley only between the two Armies, the Prince of *Orange* put his Army in Battel on two Lines, the *Spanish* Forces had the right wing, the Duke *de Villa-hermosa* commanding it; the Army of the States General the left, which the Prince of *Orange* Commanded.

Now before I speak of the Fight, which was altogether in the Valley or on its edges, I must describe the Valley. Of its length I saw no end but its breadth from one side to the other could not be less than a mile over, and of a great depth; in the bottom runs a little River, and the sides of the Valley very steep, rocky, and full of wood; no way through it where more than Horses may pass one after another, and that by turnings and windings, the Abbey of St. *Denis* is seated in it, but so low, that it is not to be seen till you come over it. On the other side the River almost opposite to St. *Dennis*, comes in a neck of Land, all plain where the Enemy had a little Camp;

the old burnt Castle of *Castio* is about two miles from St. *Denis*, seated in the Valley, and on the same side, but on a height as high as the main Land, and very near the edge of the Valley; both these places on our side, but possessed by the Enemy.

The Fight began about one of the Clock after Dinner, with the Princes planting Cannon against those Encamped on the advanced Neck of Land, and soon after fell on St. *Denis*, which was well manned, and had had many Battalions sent from the Camp on the height and *French* Army to assist it, but St. *Denis* being of no strength was quitted, and after much fighting the *French* Battalions retired to the height, the Prince's people pursuing, yet the fight continued, and bloody doings there was. About the same time the Duke *de Villa-hermosa* fell on *Castio*, and after much resistance, both from those within and the several Battalions sent from the *French* Army to its assistance, took it; yet the fight continued very warm in the

the Valley, supplyes of Battalions coming from both Armies to help theirs. Thus it held till towards the Evening. Then the *French* regained *Castio*, and their Battalions, under its covert, did not only advance to the edge of the Valley on our side, but formed two or three Battalions on the Plain. The Earl of *Ossory*, who Commanded the Foot opposite to them, did what was possible to be done, with great killing on both sides, losing most of his Officers, either killed or wounded, and himself preserved by his Arms. Whilst this was acting, and the day almost ended, two or three Squadrons of *French* Horse, sent from the Army, crossed the Valley, and coming up one after another between the Castle and their Battalions, on the sudden, and not expected, fell on the Duke *de Villahermosa*'s Guards, killing one of their Captains, with several other Officers and Soldiers, putting the rest in great disorder. The *French* Horse having done their work, and seeing more

Squadrons advancing towards them, they retired by the way they came; yet the fight continued till it was dark, and more than an hour after by the light of Houses near *Castio*, fired by the *French*. But there being no more Houses to burn, all was quiet, the *French* possessed of *Castio*, and the Battalions keeping their ground on the plain of our side, where most of the fighting had been. But about two or three hours after, Intelligence was brought that the *French* had not only quitted *Castio*, and drawn off their Battalions, but had left their Camp, and were marched towards *Monts*, and it was in great haste, for they left some Tents, and other things behind.

The Earl of *Ossory* in this afternoons work purchased to himself and noble Family immortal honor, Commanding the *English* as General in the *States* Service, and was as I believe the last man of all his Troops that came off the Field: for he was found by some of my Servants and brought

brought to me two Horses after all was ended.

The Duke of *Monmouth* was all along in this Fight, and gained as much honor as was possible for a single man, he being but a Voluntier. And I am apt to believe that if some Squadrons had charged as he desired them, that the *French* Horse that routed the Duke *de Villa-hermosa*'s Guards, would have passed their times but scurvily in their retreats. His Friend and Companion Sir *Thomas Armstrong* was shot in two or three places. It is hard to say what number of men were slain, or who lost most. I judg them on both sides to be about four or five thousand killed and wounded; among which were a number of brave Officers.

The next day, being *August* 15. there was a suspension of Arms, and ratified the 20th of the same Month. Thus with suspension of Arms we continued, till the General Peace Signed at *Nimiguen Septem.* 17. with the Ratification of it the 21th.

of *Septemb.* 1678. put an end to the Wars, tho it was said and generally believed that the Generals of both sides had the Peace in their pockets when they Fought; at least they had sufficient ground to believe it concluded.

Observe that the several dates of time in this Appendix are to be taken Stilo Novo.

Observations.

Confederate Armies joyned and acting together, tho under one *Generalissimo* are not to be esteemed equal with the Army of any Prince Commanded by one General, if the Armies are near in strength and quality.

First, All Generals of the Army that composes this Confederate Body will expect to be consulted by the *Generalissimo,* in every undertaking, that nothing may be done without their consent.

Now the bringing together these Generals; as it takes up much time, so often there follows great debates: and

The Appendix. 55

and whilſt this is doing, the Enemies Army paſſes a River or Defile, and ſometimes puts a Convoy into a place that needs it.

As for the Succouring a Town that is Beſieged where Expedition is required, there is no more compariſon in the ſpeedy Marching of theſe two Armies, than the Sailing of a ſingle Ship and a Fleet. For if any of theſe Generals do not cordially like the undertaking as ſeldom all do, tho they have in point of honor conſented, the Generals Army will come ſlowly to Rendezvouz, and then March with great Formality; drawing up at every turn, making many halts; and go over *Foot-Bridges* rather than through a Ford, where his men ſhall not be up to the knees, and might march ten abreaſt, and twenty other excuſes that I have ſeen. And many times theſe Generals do in a manner refuſe, the Orders of the *Generaliſſimo*; but ſtill cover it with ſome excuſes. Beſides, every General hath private Inſtructions from his own

own Prince. On this I conclude, that Princes Leagued ought to Act as much as possible with their Armies separated.

Secondly, Wo be to that People, whose Country is Invaded and their Prince forced to bring in Foreign Assistance, far exceeding in force, what he hath of his own Troops. These by what I have seen are worse than Enemies, set killing aside; for from these last they seek to save themselves. But Auxiliaries pretend to give Safeguards, but when the Troops of another General comes, they slight this safeguard. Thus the people Refuged in Villages, Castles, and Cloisters with all their substance, are caught in their Security; and sometimes as I have known it, does not rest with the loss of what they have, but pursued by many Sacrileges and Rapes, sparing neither Religious Women or others.

And the Army of the Country under the covert of these Strangers, being guides, do more Mischief than the

the Strangers. And sometimes this poor distressed Prince, upon pressing occasions, sends his Orders to some one or more of these Generals to march, and they will make an excuse, that they cannot get their men to it, till they have two or three months pay due to them, which must be sent if he will be served. Besides this there are many examples, where these Auxiliaries have at length Conquered the Country they came to Succour, and kept it to themselves.

Thirdly, The Security of an Army consists much in the Generals having good intelligence as well to avoid surprizes as to take advantages when occasions are offered; for there is no Army but sometimes in Marching or Camping is exposed to the Enemy, if they knew all and the time for taking their advantage.

Fourthly, A General whose condition is to seek fighting must be careful how he brings his Army too near the Enemy well posted, without he comes with resolution to force him in his Camp,

Camp, or that he can Encamp so by him at his ease as the Enemy must be enforced to march off before him. For otherwise, at his going off, he will run great risk of being dangerously attacted in the Flank, Rear, or both; especially if it be where there are Defiles or Rivers.

Fifthly. A General that Marches with an Army for the Succour of a Town, Besieged by another as great, or near as powerful as that which he Commands, if the Enemy on his approach draws off, and puts himself in Battel out of his way, or is Marching clear off, the General having gained his point, is not to take notice of him, but without losing time to furnish the wants of the Town, make up the Breaches, destroy the Lines and Trenches made by the Enemy. For if this General pursue and in fighting have the better, 'tis but some addition to his Glory; but if beaten, he loses his Army, Town, and Honor: for an Enemy may be willing to fight having drawn off, which he dare

dare not do holding the Siege.

Sixthly. A General that fights an Army of which he knows the ſtrength, hath great advantage of another General that fights he knows not what, as it appeared in the Battel of *Caſtlet.* For the Duke of *Orleans* might know almoſt to a man, with what ſtrength the Prince of *Orange* could come; but the Prince of *Orange* could not know that of him, whilſt the King of *France* was ſo near, at the Siege of *Cambray,* who with his whole Army might have joyned the Duke of *Orleans* as eaſily as the Detachment did.

Seventhly. A General that hath his Magazines fully ſtored with all neceſſaries, and well placed in order to his deſign, having the advantage of Rivers, and no want of Wagons, may well Beſiege a Town ſeated near thoſe Rivers in all ſeaſons of the year, and with more advantage in the Winter, or rather in the Spring, before there be Forrage, than afterwards. For the Enemy that might be feared to March for the Succour muſt have time

time to bring his Army together, and then not having the conveniencies of Rivers be forced to bring all his Provisions by Land in Wagons. And it is almost impossible, if his Magazines and Country be far off, to supply his Army with Forrage, being to be brought at so great a distance. And if the Army with this Winter doing be weakned and shattered, the Sieges being over, and Forrage coming on, it will soon recover, or at least be able to make a defensive War, for the preservation of Towns that must be attacked in form, and then towards the latter end of the year being recruited and recovered act again.

8. An Army marching and making halts whilst ways are mending, or Bridges making, is not without apprehension, and danger, if the Enemy's Army be not far off. To avoid this, when the General hath taken his Resolution to march, and by what way, and on how many Colomes or Lines, he immediatly sends trusty and knowing Officers with a good

good Escourt of Horse and Foot with Pioneers to mend, and make clear the ways for the March; and if there be Rivers, Boats for Bridges; then putting good guides with the Officer Commanding each Line, he marches without interruption. But great care is to be taken that the Lines march equal, and not too far asunder, that so they may (in case of an Alarm) be found, or put easily in order of Battel.

9. Troops pressed in Fight do incline much to croud in one upon another; so that if you have not Field room it is hard to untangle, and put them in order. In that case, sometimes it may be wished that half the number were away.

10. In Battels it ought to be held as an undoubted maxim of War, that a Wing of Horse beating the Enemies opposite Wing, is not to move one Foot in the pursuit, but to keep its first order, and if the Rout be such that the Enemies ought to be pursued, let it be done by Detachments

or

or commanded men, and if the Battel be gained, no plundring till all be secured.

I do not absolutely reject Battels: for in some cases they are to be fought, and in others tho a General do not seek fighting, yet he must expose his Army to Battel, if the Enemy will. But certainly it is a matter of great consideration, especially when a Country is Invaded: for the loss of a Battel is many times the loss of a Kingdom. And let a General be never so great a Captain, having ranged his Army in the best manner, and given to his Officers all good Orders; yet when the Armies are once engaged, he can act little more than one mans part, and is subject by the failure of many others to be overthrown.

12. Towns are for the most part Besieged because of defects in their Fortifications, or wants within, as Men, Ammunition, or Provisions, &c. so as to keep out these reliefs, as also fence the quarters, a Line of Circumvallation is very necessary; and till
it

it be put in defence neither Horse nor Foot are to pretend any rest, or any Trench to be opened. But when all is done, if a considerable Army come to post it self near this Line, if it be not very good and well Flanked, with a good Ditch and Parapet, no ground to Command it, and men sufficient to Man it besides those in the Trenches, carrying on the attacks, it is better to hazard a Battel in a plain Field than to fight behind such a Line. For the Enemy lying by you is commonly strongly posted, will annoy your Convoys and Forragers, if this will not make you raise your Siege. And if the Town be worth it, he will take his time to attempt your Line by force, and begins commonly an hour or two before day, alarming you round; falls on with some false attacks, and two or three real ones. Your Line is often fifteen or twenty miles about; and if a River runs by the Town, as for the most part there does, this Line is divided, and so your Army has no Communication but by Bridges of Boats. And in this case it being dark, none goes to help the other; but every one stands to defend his part of the Line, none knowing where the real danger is, but he that feels it. And if there be a Camp Volant, with the General, he may with it march wrong as well as right: and the Enemy once entred, usually all quit the Line, and seek to save themselves; and it is hard to put them in any order of Battel to resist; so that all can be hoped for, is to make a reasonable retreat. Now in case the Enemy fail in their attempt, they run little or no hazard: for they retire before it be full day, and those within the Line dare hardly pursue till Parties sent out in the morning to discover return. Now if you draw out, and fighting, gain a Battel, tho a relief whilst you are engaged, slip into the place, those within seeing their Succour beaten, lose courage, and in all likelihood will give you little trouble before they render.

13. A General coming before a Town with a design to Besiege it, must be well informed of all things within and without before he opens his Trenches. For I have seen by the mistake of the true attack much time trifled away with the loss of many Lives, and I think once with the Defeat of the whole Army.

14. A General that in a retreat brings his Army to attempt the passing a River or great Defile, an Enemies Army being near, or in view, runs too much hazard, if it be not by necessity, and then he is blameable to have brought it to the extremity.

15. The passing of Defiles and Rivers may be attempted, an Enemies Army near or looking on, in certain cases; as for the Succor of a Town or breaking into an Enemies Country to Conquer. The reason of this, is chiefly grounded in the difference of mens Courages and Resolutions in attacking, or being attacked. For as a retreat looks something like runing away, especially to the Common

Soldiers, so advancing, raises them to confidence of overcoming. Store of Cannon in this case is of great use, but a General having passed with his Army these Rivers or Defiles, and being to return the same way, or by other Rivers, or Defiles, must be careful to leave the Passes well secured for his retreat; otherwise after all, if the Enemy seizes the Passes or Defiles behind him, he may in part or in the whole lose his Army. Now as the passing of Rivers and Defiles are dangerous, so there ought to be great consideration in the opposition, and not to put wholly the fortune of a weaker Army upon it. For if the Enemy force the Pass, in all likelihood you shall be beaten. Wherefore in this case, if you will oppose, put your Army in Battel as much covered from Cannon as you can, improving the Enemies Disorder, what you may, and as they arrive on your side of the Pass, Charge, not suffering them to Form.

16. Great

16. Great advantages in War are rarely offered, and for the most part soon past. Wherefore tho patience and circumspection are vertues in a General, or Chief Commander; yet they ought to be watchful, and hold their Troops so ready that they may not lose the critical minute or precious moment; it being of so much importance in War, that the like peradventure may not happen in the life of a man. I have seen my self in two or three occasions a Victory gained, that if one quarter of an hour had been omitted in the attempt, the Fortune of the day in all likelihood had gone quite contrary to what it did. The cause is clear, and found by experience. For tho man in his Reason be the most excellent of all creatures on earth; yet having lost it by the passion of Fear, is one of the least; and fear doth sometimes seize men being in surprize to such a degree that they know not what they do.

How many men in beating up Quarters and Routs are slain, not daring

ring to turn their faces to make refiftance; tho the very fame men being, in their judgments, in divers occafions had carried themfelves formerly well enough.

17. No Merchant ought to be more exact in his Books than a General in keeping account of the Enemies Provifions, how they are brought to the Army, and the days, that fo he may take his advantage.

18. A General muft be very wary how he engages his Army in the Siege of a Town, or Invades an Enemies Country, chiefly relying on a Party within the Town, or a rifing of the People in his favor. I have feen and known fatal confequences in both, even to the lofs of Armies; yet fometimes it hath fucceeded. However, the offers of Enemies, or of thofe that live amongft them, are ftill to be fufpected.

19. A Prince in time of War ought to be large in rewarding, and very fevere in punifhing. His General, whilft he is fo, is to be abfolute, and the
Prince

Prince not apt to hear complaints against him. That there be from the General, even to the Corporle throughout the whole Army an entire and known subordination, that, each may know whom he is to command, and whom to obey. Also, that the Troops of the Army may as near as possible be on the same foot, and payed alike.

Yet in the King of *Spains Netherlands,* for what reason of State or War I could never learn, there are many important cases undetermined; as between Generals *de Battalia,* and Governors of Provinces, in the Province under their Government who should command; the General *de Battalia* coming into the Province with an Army, or Party, or with orders to command a Town.

Of the National Regiments, which are in those Countries, few or none will give place to the other; from whence arise (sometimes) dangerous contests even in the face of the Enemy.

One General *de Battalia* will not obey another.

The same amongst Maisters de Camps of Foot and Collonels of Foot.

Maisters de Camps of Horse and Colonels of Horse contest with those of the Foot; as also amongst themselves.

Captains of Horse and Majors of Foot contest.

In fine, there is room left for dispute even amongst the Common Soldiers of several Nations.

20. The person of a successfull General, beloved by the Army, and in high esteem for his experience and Conduct in War, is highly to be valued. For the Soldiers believe that with this man they cannot be beaten, and with another of contrary Reputation they are always in doubt. The same holds in proportion with the inferior Commanders. I have seen the effect of this both in Armies and Parties.

21. An Army is more to be valued for its quality, and readiness to Action, than for its number.

22. The

22. The Defects of an Army.

As Generals and other Commanders not of Reputation and Experience in War.

The Troops compofed for the moſt part of new men.

The Horfe was well mounted.

Neither Horfe nor Foot well armed.

The Officers for want of pay not valuing their imployments; and the Soldiers in a Mutinous humor for the fame caufe.

Defects and Wants in the Artillery and its Train.

Great difference is to be made between Victorious and Cow'd or Beaten Troops, till the latter be recovered by fome good Winter-Quarters, or other Forces joyn them.

23. A Body of Horfe retired into a weak place is never to be thought fafe; if an Enemies Army be within

a days March of them; for once Invested, they are lost.

22, Languishing Sieges are to be avoided; for tho an Army comes at first with much Resolution and Courage, and so holds it on for a time they think convenient for taking such a place; yet when they see the General doth not advance the attacks as he ought, and they lose men by sharp Sallies; sometimes the Cannon nayled, and the Lodging of the night before broken down, their Convoys cut; report of an Army Marching for its succour; ill weather coming on; and sometimes a small relief slipping into the Town, which can hardly be avoided till a place be closely blocked; these, and many other accidents, which Armies at a Siege are subject to, make men cool, and often desert, to the weakening of an Army; that when the Enemies Army appears, they will be found nothing of what they were at first. Therefore I conclude, that reasonable hazarding to make dispatch is the saving

ving of men, and the surest way of taking a Town.

25. The Confederate Armies Commanded by the Prince of *Orange* as Generalissimo (most of them present at the Battel of *Seneff*, and Siege of *Audenard*,) were the Emperors, Commanded by the Count *de Souch*; the King of *Spain*'s first by the Count *de Monterey*, afterwards by the Duke *de Villa-hermosa*, both Governors of *Flanders*; that of the *States General*, Commanded by the Count *de Waldeck*; that of the Prince and Bishop of *Osnaburgh*, by Monsieur *Lovigny*; the Marquess of *Brandenburgh*'s, by Monsieur *Spaune*; that of *Luningbourgh* and *Zelle*, by Monsieur *Chouet*; the Army of *Munster*, by the Baron *de Wedle*.

POST

POSTSCRIPT.

IT might with reason long since have been expected that I should have published something in my own Vindication, having been extremely ill treated in a long Letter I received from the Earl of *Anglesey* then Lord Privy-Seal, which Letter his Lordship soon after thought fit to expose to the view of the World in Print; but my good Fortune was that his Lordship by an unnecessary digression fell foul on the Duke of *Ormond* and others, for which being questioned, his Lordship suffered in a high degree..

As to my self I shall only note three or four things, his Lordship begins his Letter to me Folio the first.

My Lord Castlehaven.

Having received your Lordships Letter of the 24th. currant with your printed Memoirs which you are pleased in some sort to intitle me to; here

POSTSCRIPT.

I muſt ſay how I came to ſend this Letter of the 24th. currant with the Memoirs.

The Earl of *Angleſey* from his houſe near *Oxford*, I being in *London*, ſent me a ſhort Letter, deſiring me to ſend him one of my Memoirs: In anſwer to this I ſent him the mentioned of the 24th. currant, all written with my own hand, telling him in it that there was no ſuch thing in nature as my Memoirs; but gueſſing at his meaning I ſent him one of the Books I ſuppoſe he meant, telling him how it came into my hands, but diſowning and proteſting againſt the Book. Now if my Lord of *Angleſey* ſhall not think fit to produce this Letter being it will ſhew too much his fondneſs to writing; yet I do undertake when called upon, to make out by undoubted teſtimony, that I diſowned thoſe Books when they firſt came to light and proteſted againſt them.

Folio 7. and 8. His Lordſhip makes my Story of two parts, as having ſerved by the Confederate Catholicks

POSTSCRIPT.

licks Commiſſion till the Ceſſation made with the Marqueſs of *Ormond* concluded *Septemb.* 15. 1643. All which time ſaith he your Lordſhip was wholly of the Rebels Party and under their Pay and Command; the ſecond part from that time till your Lordſhip finding the ill ſtate of affairs in *Ireland,* was diſpatched by the then Lord Deputy *Clanrickard* to ſet out the ſame to the King in *France* which was in the year 51. tho his Lordſhip doth not mark it. Here this noble Lord ſhews himſelf ill informed in what paſs'd in *Ireland* in thoſe days; for in the year (44) it is notoriouſly known that I Commanded an Army in *Ulſter* againſt the *Scots* by Commiſſion from the Confederate Catholicks.

And the following year (45) by Commiſſion from the ſame perſons I Commanded another Army in *Munſter* againſt my Lord of *Inchiquin.*

In the ſame page of (8.) he ſaith, My Lord I am loth now to make my Remarques upon this ſecond part, becauſe

POSTSCRIPT.

cause your Lordship Acting therein at times under the Confederate-*Irish* their Commission, and under his Majesties Authority at other times, and sometimes under both; these assertions are so untrue that I wonder where his Lordship hath picked up his Information; for it may be seen on Records that I served by the Confederate Catholicks their Commission till the Peace of (46.)

And then having laid hold on the Kings Mercy, always since have owned no other Authority but his, and am sorry for the time past.

His Lordship spake of a Feast which I had prepared for the Lord of *Mungarret* and the Rebels; but the Marquess of *Ormond* having gained the Battel at *Killrush* ate that I could not keep from him.

Now this is as poor an aspersion as 'tis untrue, for the Duke of *Ormond* knows the contrary, so doth many more yet alive, for hardly could it be called a tolerable meal but to men that were hungry.

I shall

POSTSCRIPT.

I shall trouble the Reader with no more on this Subject, but conclude that my Lord of *Angleseys* long Printed Letter is all along subject to mistakes, speaking Modestly.

FINIS.

ERRATA.

Page 16. Line 7. Read *find it.* p. 17. l. 1. r. *heads.* p. 19. l. 8. r. *Premises.* p. 42. r. *Canon.* p. 47. r. *Loftus.* p. 48. l. 16. r. *that.* p. 57. l. 5. r. *touching.* p. 60. l. 16. r. *Scarampus.* p. 61. l. 18. r. *too.* and l. 26. r. *cull'd.* p. 64. l. 21. r. *Clanmaleer.* p. 65. l. 23. r. *Served.* l. 26. *Balla-Lenan.* p. 69. l. 6. r. *too.* p. 76. l. 16. r. *where they.* p. 113. l. 4. r. *concerning.* p. 119. l. 3. dele *other.* p. 123. l. 17. r. *Athlone.* p. 169. l. 20. r. *too.*

In the Appendix.

Page 3. Line 13. read *hindering.* p. 6. l. 6. r. *to Paris.* p. 21. l. 5. r. *Dermond.* p. 22. l. 25. r. *the.* p. 53. l. 1. r. *hours.*

A LETTER

From a Person of HONOUR in the COUNTREY Written to the EARL of CASTLEHAVEN.

BEING

Observations and Reflections Upon his Lordships MEMOIRES Concerning the WARS of IRELAND.

LONDON,

Printed for *Nath. Ponder* at the *Peacock* in the *Poultrey*, 1681.

A LETTER

Written to the EARL of CASTLEHAVEN.

My Lord Castlehaven,

HAving Received your Lordships of the 24th Current, with your printed Memoires, which you are pleased in some sort to Intitle me to; and I will not conceal from your Lordship that I am not yet ashamed, now I have read them, though I cannot approve all in them, that I was the first incentive to your Writing them; which was upon this occasion, having sat along with your Lordship in Parliament, and obſerving for the moſt part ſuch a conſent between your Lordſhip and me, in proceedings there upon the moſt abſtracted Principles of Honour and Allegiance, I could not but account of your Lordſhip as a true Engliſhman and a Loyal Subject, whatſoever blemiſh your engagement under the confederate Rebels of *Ireland* had before fixed on you; and having heard you ſo often pathetically declare your ſelf fully to mine and moſt honeſt Mens Minds, againſt the dangers of the growing greatneſs of the *French* and the too faſt Declenſion of the *Spaniard*, between which great Powers of the World, the Crown of *England* was ſo happy and wiſe in former times as to hold and guide the Ballance; and finding by your frequent, and as I could not but conceive, Cordial Expreſſions againſt the Pope of *Rome*'s Uſurping Authority in theſe Dominions, over and againſt his Majeſty, and Kingdoms, to ſuch a degree,

gree, that you spared not, like a right Ancient Peer of this Realm, often to say, That if the Pope himself should Attack any of his Majesties Dominions, you would be one of the first to labour his Destruction; I was deservedly much delighted in your Lordships Converse: which having been often honoured with, both by your Letters, when in Foreign parts, and your favourable Society here at home, I was instrumental, as your Lordship well knows, to prevail with the Parliament to set a mark of great Honour on your Lordship, by a special recommendation and intercession to his Majesty for a regard to and reparation of the Breaches time and misfortune had made upon so Ancient and Honourable a Family. And looking upon your Lordship as a Peer of most noble Principles, and free of the worst part of Bigotry, I could not but lament your leaving the Parliament, and still wish your return.

During our said Converse, being ingaged in the History of *Ireland*, to which I was the more inclined by an interest therein for several Generations; my Great Grandfather, Sir *John Perrot*, having been Deputy thereof, governing the same with great Wisdom and Success, my Grandfather *Annesley* having been Commander at Sea in Queen *Elizabeths* time, and one of the Undertakers for Land in *Munster*, after the Earl of *Desmond* s Rebellion; my Father, the Lord Baron of *Mountnorris*, and Viscount of *Valentia* (of whom I have very often heard your Lordship speak with great Honour, and as your worthy Friend) having faithfully served King *James* and King *Charles* the First, near Forty years in that Kingdom, in Offices and Imployments of high Trust; and I my self being a Native of the City of *Dublin*, a diligent Observer of the Troubles there, wherein I had some share; and having both Honours and Lands

de-

descended to me in that Realm; and knowing that your Lordship had heretofore a great part in the Action there, and taking notice that no Memorials I had yet seen, did give a full account of your Lordship, whom as my own Friend and my Fathers Friend, I was willing to do right to in History, as far as I could; ever highly esteeming the Bravery of your Actions and Wisdom of your Conduct, as far as I had Cognizance thereof, though I *bemoaned* the unhappy circumstances of your engaging under a Power usurping over your own Prince, and incroaching Royal Power; which I find you cannot digest, either the Pope or Duke of *Lorraine* should have done: I discoursed with your Lordship many of the most important Designs, Actions and Traverses of Fortune in *Ireland*, since the fatal 23 of *October* 1641, and finding by your full Relations, with a perfect memory thereof, that you were able to give help to History therein;

therein; I moved your Lordſhip (to which you friendly conſented) that at leaſure hours you would reduce to writing what you could remember, with as exact reference to Time and Order (as you could recollect) of Paſſages and Exploits there; and that I might by your favour be poſſeſſed thereof: And I wiſh things had reſted there, little expecting a formal Relation in print, and much leſs ſo introduced before I had the peruſal of it; for I muſt now acquaint your Lordſhip, that I did not, after what I have above related, ſave now and then to your ſelf, inquire after your Memoires promiſed me, till by a Letter of the 16th of this moneth, from a hand I reſpect, I had notice he had ſeen them; and my Cenſure thereon was deſired, they ſeeming to him (after 28 years ſilence, to caſt a Calumny on the Government then; and as he ſuſpects, with no good intention, though he refers that to my Opinion; knowing (as he is
pleaſed

pleased to say) none to appeal to but me. Your Lordship sees now how you are ingaged for want of commanding my Service before the Printers: and I am confident the heat of a Battle would be less formidable to you then the Paper warre you must expect to be assaulted with; wherein, if I be necessitated to have the least hand, your Lordship may be assured it shall be *en Gentilhome & en amy*, and chiefly with an aim to convince your Lordship of that which hath obscured the Glory of your Adventures and Exploits or Undertakings, in that unfortunate Kingdom; and therefore I forbear giving any Opinion to my Friend, till I have vented my thoughts to your Lordship, which I shall now take the liberty to do.

Upon serious perusal of your Book, I find your Lordships Story of two parts, The First till the Cessation of Arms concluded by the Rebels Commissioners at *Seginstowne*, with the

Marquess

Marquess of *Ormond*, *Sept.* 15, 1643; all which time your Lordship was wholly of the Rebels Party, and under their Pay and Command, which I wish your Lordship had not thought fit for the Press, though there were some Acts of Souldierly bravery in it. The Second Part, From that time till your Lordship finding the ill state of Affairs in *Ireland*, was dispatched by the then Lord Deputy *Clanrickord*, to set out the same to the King in *France*; from whence, though your Lordship procured a Letter from his Majesty to the Lord Deputy, and sent the same by a safe Messenger, yet you returned not again, but ingaged in the Service of the Prince of *Conde*. My Lord, I am loath now to make my Remarques upon this Second Part, because your Lordships acting therein at times, under the Confederate Irish their Commission, and under his Majesties Authority at other times, and sometimes under both.

It

It will be fitter at present for me to be silent therein, than to attempt the unblending such a mixture, and seperate your Acts of Allegiance from those of Opposition to the King, which I must always blame you for: or to condemn you intirely, when some things your Lordship did were by full Authority, though very fatal to the English Protestant interest in that Kingdom, and no ways advantagious to his Majesty or his Affairs.

But the First Part of your Story, which takes up three Sections of your Memoirs, I cannot let pass unanimadverted and corrected, without condemning the generation of the just; suffering Blemish, and Calumny, to lie upon his Majesty and Government, both in *England* and *Ireland*; and leaving your Lordship in a mistake of having done well, when I hope I shall evince that you did very ill, unless the galantry of a Souldier can expiate for all that was amiss. For this end

I must take notice to your Lordship, that all I find you urge to satisfie your own Conscience, or to vindicate your Honour and Integrity to the World, in this your ingaging your self amongst the Irish, is to this effect: Your Lordship saith, That at the first eruption of the Rebellion (which you seem to tye to the North, but was universal) you acquainted the Lords Justices with your willingness to serve the King against the Rebels, as your Ancestors had formerly done in *Ireland*; but they replying, that your Religion was an Obstacle; there being then a Parliament in that Kingdom sitting, you were resolved to see the event, sending your Brother to your House at *Madingstowne*, in the County of *Kildare*, to secure and defend it, in case there were any rising in those parts. Sometime after the Parliament being dissolved (but you do not mention that you attended your duty in Parliament, when it was sitting, and

declaring

declaring against the Rebels) your Lordship desired a Pass from the Justices to go to *England*, but they refusing, you acquainted them with the condition of your Estate, and desired a supply of Money till you could apply to the Parliament of *England* for a Pass to bring you over, which they denyed. You press'd them then to direct you what course you should steer, to which they replied, Go home and make fair weather. You took this advice, and being come, my Lord of *Antrim*, and my Lady Dutchess of *Buckingham* (both Papists and after that deeply ingaged in the Rebellion) soon followed (whether by concert with your Lordship is not said) and you were very well pleased with so good company. But in a short time the Irish came and drove away great part of your Stock, which you recovered by a party sent out with your Brother, who brought with him two or three of the chiefest Conductors of

that

that Rabble. This inraged the Irish so much, as you conceived your Brother was not safe there, and therefore sent him to *Dublin*, to attend the Justices Orders, and assure them of your readiness to return on a call, they sending a Convoy, which they promised to do as Occasion required. But your Lordship hearing that you were indicted of High Treason, and hereupon your Brother addressing to the Lords Justices again, to let them know that they had not kept their words with him, in suffering this clandestine proceeding against you (as your Brothers Letter calls it) you went to *Dublin*, and addressed your self to my Lord of *Ormond*, as your Brother did in your behalf to the Lords Justices and Council, to acquaint them with your coming; and upon your appearance before them they ordered you to come the day following, at which time, without calling you in, they committed you to
Mr.

Mr. *Woodcock's* House, one of the Sheriffs of *Dublin*. Your Brother seeing (as he calls it) this rigorous usage towards you, and being refused a Pass for himself to go for *England*, he got away to the King at *York*, and petitioned him that you might be sent for over to be tryed here by your Peers. But his Majesties Answer was, That he had left all the Affairs of *Ireland* to the Parliament; upon which he petitioned the Parliament to the same effect: their Answer was, that they could do nothing without the King. After this your Brother saith, he was continually serving his Majesty in *England*. Your Lordship once more placeth your self at *Madenstowne*, whither you had at first retired by advice of the Lords Justices, and continued there some Five or six moneths after in peace and quietness; but your Lordship doth not mention that other neighbouring places possessed by the English did so; or what intelligence your

your Lordship had with or gave to the State. But proceed to say, That in the mean while Parties were sent out by the Justices from *Dublin*, and the Towns adjacent, to kill and destroy the Rebels; and the like was done through all parts of the Kingdom. But your Lordship adds, the Officers and Souldiers did not take care enough to distinguish between the Rebels and Subjects, but killed in many places promiscuously; on which partly, and partly on other provocations that proceeded, and some too that followed, the whole Nation finding themselves concerned, took to Arms for their own defence, and particularly the Lords of the Pale did so, who yet at the same time desired the Justices to send their Petition to the King, which was refused. And for their further discouragement, Sir *John Read*, his Majesties sworn Servant (a stranger to the Countrey, uningaged, and an Eyewitness of their proceedings, then upon

upon his Journey to *England*) prevailed with by them, to carry their Remonstrance to his Majesty, and to beg his Pardon for what they had done; coming to *Dublin*, and not concealing his Message, was put to the Rack for his good will. The said Lords having tryed this and other ways to acquaint the King with their Grievances, and all failing, an open War broke forth generally throughout the Kingdom. Your Lordship next takes notice of your accidental entertaining my Lord of *Ormond* at Dinner, immediately after the Battle of *Killrush*, which you were a Spectator of, being in sight of your House; but that some who came with him, turned this another way, and publishing through the Army, that it was a mighty Feast for my Lord *Mount Garret* and the Rebels; this through the English Quarters past for currant. And you believe it was much the cause of this under-hand villainous proceedings (as you call it) against you fore-mentioned. Your Lordship proceeds to tells us, That after Twenty Weeks that you had remained in Prison, you were ordered to be removed to the Castle of *Dublin*, which startled you, and brought to your thoughts the proceedings against the Earl of *Strafford*, who confiding in his Innocency, lost his Head: you concluded then that Innocency was a scurvey plea in an angry time; besides, your Lordship looked upon the Justices and most of the Council to be of the Parliaments Perswasion; wherefore you resolved to attempt an escape, and save your self in the Irish Quarters, which your Lordship did, and give us a Relation of the manner of it; and how your Lordship took your way towards the Mountains of *Wicklow*, where being come, you cared little for the Justices, though before Dinner, your escape being discovered, on notice given to the Justices, you were pursued by a party of of Horse, taking their way to your House at *Madingstowne*, which they invested in the night: but not finding your Lordship, after possessing themselves of what your Lordship had within and without, they killed many of your Servants and burnt the House. Your Lordship kept on your way to *Kilkenny*, as much through the Fast Countrey as you could, till you arrived, where you found the Town very full, and many of your acquaintance, all preparing for their Natural Defence; seeing no distinction made, or safety but in Arms. To this end your Lordship saith, They had chosen amongst themselves, out of the most eminent Persons, a Council, and gave it the Title of, *The Supream Council of the Confederate Catholicks of* Ireland; and formed an Oath of Association, by which all were bound to obey them. They had made Four Generals of the Four Provinces, *Preston* of *Leinster*, *Barry* of *Munster*, Owen-Roe Oneil of *Ulster*, and one *Burk* of *Connaught*; and being to give Commiſſions, they cauſed a Seal to be made, which was the Seal of the Council. Your Lordſhip ſaith, you were ſent for to this Council to tell your Story, which you did. And being asked what you intended to do, you anſwered, to get into *France*, and ſo to *England*; upon which they told you their condition, and what they were doing for their preſervation, perſwading you to ſtay with them, being your Lordſhip was beloved in the Countrey; had three Siſters married amongſt them, was perſecuted upon the ſame ſcore they were, and ruined; ſo that you had no more to loſe but your Lives. You took two or three days to think of this Propoſition, examining the Medel of Government they had prepared againſt the meeting of the general Aſſembly, and moſt particularly their Oath of Aſſociation, which your Lordſhip judged to be very reaſonable, as the caſe ſtood. On

On the whole matter you returned to this Council, Thanked them for their good Opinion of you, and engaged your self to run a Fortune with them. Whether Anger and Revenge did not incline you to it as much as any other consideration, you say you cannot resolve; but this you well remember, that you considered how you had been used, and seen your House burning as you passed by; besides, that you were a light man, with no charge, and not any hopes of redress from the King, who was then engaged in an intestine War. Now being thus a Confederate, and having taken the Oath, they made your Lordship one of the Council, and General of the Horse under *Preston*.

The Assemby met the 24th of *October*, 1642. It differed nothing from a Parliament, other then that the Lords and Commons sate together, and not in two Houses.

This your Lordship saith, we see was a force-put upon you, and you hoped in time, the storm being passed, to return to your old Government under the King. You had many Learned in the Law amongst you, whom you incouraged to keep you as near the Old Government as might be; holding to the Ancient Laws of the Land.

That Assemby, without delay, approved all the Council had done, and settled a Model of Government, *viz.* That at the end of every General Assembly, the Supreme Council should be Confirmed or Changed as they thought fit. That it should consist of Twenty five, six out of each Province, three of the six still Resident.

The 25th was your Lordship, with no Relation to any Province, but to the Kingdom in general. Every Province had a Provincial Assembly, which met on occasions, and each Countrey had Commissions for Applotting Money within themselves, as it came to their shares, upon the general Applotment

of

of the Province. Many other things there were as to Government. If a better came to them written in Irish, it would be wondred at, and hardly could one be found to read it. You say you were not in case to bring to Justice those that begun the Rebellion. But you never saw any of them esteemed or advanced. The general Assembly being put off, the Generals fell to their work, and your Lordships General took in *Burras*, Fort *Faukland* and *Burrish*, in the *Kings County*, where you were with him. Your Lordship was also with this General the 18th of *March*, 1642, when he was beaten at *Ross* by the Marquess of *Ormond*, and by Collonel *Monk*, since Duke of *Albermarle*, at *Timochoe*, in the *Queens County*, the Fifth of *October*, 1642. Yet afterwards he besieging *Ballynekill*, in the same County, you ventured once more with him; where he having intelligence that Major General *Crawford* was

was Besieging *Ballybritas*, a Castle, belonging to the Viscount *Clanmalleer*, he sent your Lordship with a party of Fifteen hundred Horse and Foot, to endeavour the succouring of that place, which your Lordship did; and *Crawford* drawing off, in passing the River of the *Barrow*, in a Skirmish, had his Thigh broken with a Musket Shot. You returned as *Ballynekill* was rendred. After this your Lordship remained at *Kilkenny*, with the Supream Council, and *Preston* went into the lower parts of the Province with the Army; of whose Absence, the Enemies Garrisons, in the County of *Catherlagh* and *Queens County*, taking advantage, allarm'd the County of *Kilkenny*, even to the Gates of the City. Your Lordship was then by the Council commanded to go against them. And therefore having gotten together about 2000 Men, with some Cannon, you marched to *Ballynunry*, in the County of *Catherlagh*, and took

took it; as also *Cloghgrenan*, where the County of *Wexford*'s Regiment mutined, but were reduced and some Examples made, served well for the future. Your Lordship marched thence into the *Queens County*, and Besieged *Bellylenan*, Commanded by the *Grimes*'s, a valiant People, with a strong Garrison. But a great breach being made, their Succour came by the way of *Athy*. Your Lordship was not well at this Allarm, but laid upon your Bed in your Tent. However you made no great matter of it, knowing the Succour could not be considerable; but your Lordship beating their Succour in their view, the besieged Garrison yielded, on condition to march out with their Arms. And then your Lordship was perswaded to head the *Munster* Forces, of whose Success, under your Command, you give a full Relation; and then returning to *Kilkenny*, gave the Assembly an account of what had passed. Soon after the Assembly

Aſſembly being broke up, and a Supream Council choſen to govern in their abſence; you retired to *Kilkaſh*, your Brother *Butler's* Houſe, to reſt your ſelf. The Council went to *Roſs*, and whilſt they were there, a Trumpet brought them a Letter from the Marqueſs of *Ormond*, ſetting forth his being appointed by the King to hear your Grievances, and to treat for an accommodation. The particulars of the Letter you know not, but the Trumpet was quickly diſpatched with ſome ſlight Anſwer; which coming to your knowledge, you repaired to *Kilkenny*, whither the Council was returned; and on information, finding what you had heard to be true, you ſent for Sir *Bobert Talbot*, Sir *Richard Barnwall*, Collonel *Walter Bagnal*, and ſuch others as were in the Town, well affected and leading Men of the Aſſembly, though not of the Council. Now being in your Lodging, you acquainted them with what you had underſtood, and

and that if they would stick to you, you would endeavour to give it a turn. You all agreed on the way, which was to go to the Council then sitting, to take notice of the Kings offer, and their return; and to mind them that the confideration and refolutions concerning Peace and War, the general Affembly referved to themfelves only; and therefore to require that they would fend immediately a Trumpet of their own, with a Letter to the Marquefs of *Ormond*, giving him to underftand they had iffued a Summons for a general Affembly, in order to acknowledge the Kings gracious Favour, in naming him his Commiffioner to hear your Aggrievances and redrefs them. This you put in execution, and gained your point without much refiftance.

The Marquefs of *Ormond* being thus brought into a Treaty, the Confederate Commiffioners met at *Seginftowne*, near the *Naffe*, as his Excellency

lency had appointed, in order to a Cessation of Arms. At which time all Parties laboured to get into possession of what they could. Collonel *Monk*, after made Duke of *Albermarle*, march'd into the County of *Wicklow* to take in the Harvest, and possess some Castles. Your Lordship being then commanded by the Council to go against him, and having Rendevouz'd your Troops, consisting of about 3000 Horse and Foot at *Ballynekill*, in the County of *Catherlagh*; notice was brought you that Collonel *Monk* was marched away in all haste to the assistance of the Lord *Moor*, then facing *Owen Roe Oneal*, near *Portlester*. You finding your self now to have nothing to do, thought it worth the while to endeavour taking in *Dullerstown*, *Tully*, *Lacagh*, and all other Castles in the County of *Kildare*, between the Rivers of the *Barrow* and *Liffe*, which you did; leaving Garrisons in them. This done, you repast

past the *Barrow* at *Monaster-Evan*, marched into *Leix*, and took three or four small places. But as you were going on, had Advice from the Commissioners at *Seginstowne*, that they had on the 15th of *September*, 1643, concluded a Cessation of Arms with the Marquess of *Ormond*, to which you submited.

As your Lordship did also to the two Peaces of 1646, 1648, both sutable, and of the same strain; and though both were of advantage only to the *Irish*, and highly dishonourable to the Crown of *England*, and destructive to the *English* and *Protestants*, yet both were broken and set at naught by the *Irish* themselves, a just Judgment of God against them, whose hands were full of Blood; and there being no hopes that such untempered Morter could cement them and the Posterity left alive of murdered Parents, Brothers, Sisters, and other Relations; or that ever the *English* could

could live out of danger, and free of Maſſacres for the future, without exemplary puniſhment of the Murderers and Rebels, and bringing them by forfeitures and otherwiſe, to an abſolute ſubjection to the Laws, and keeping them in that ſtate. as it is now hoped they are, and will be by the watchful Eye of Government.

I ſhall now, as briefly as I can, take the liberty to give your Lordſhip impartial Remarks upon what your Lordſhip hath written In juſtification of the Rebels, or tending to caluminate his Majeſties Government, or Engliſh and Proteſtant Subjects; reſerving a fuller account thereof to a fitter occaſion.

In the firſt place, Seeing your Lordſhips *Memoires*, dedicated to the King, I cannot but take notice how dangerous a thing it is, and of how bad conſequence it may prove, eſpecially in this caſe and juncture, to miſinform his Majeſty; not that I do ſuſpect or tax your Lordſhip of deſign to abuſe the

the King; for I do charitably believe, as your Lordship affirms upon your word, that they do not contain a lie or mistake to your knowledge, yet I must positively aver, and it is my part to make it good, that the Relation wants the most material and pregnant Truths in the principal part thereof, and of most consequence to the Publick, as I doubt not your Lordship will believe and confess upon such glances as I shall make upon particulars as I go over them. But before I proceed, it will import the giving clear light to an affair, which contrary interests have so much endeavoured to perplex, to observe the state that unhappy Kingdom of *Ireland* was in at the Eruption of that fatal Rebellion. A Parliament sitting the year before in *Ireland*, both Houses taking notice of some Grievances growing upon them, and the want of some good New Laws for advancing the Prosperity and good Government of that Kingdom, did

did send chosen Agents or Commissioners, both Lords and Commons, of most esteem amongst them, to attend his Majesty in *England*, for redress of such Grievances, and procuring such new Grants and Graces, as they were directed to move for, from a Gracious King. His Majesty received them favourably and with good dispatch, they returned for *Ireland* fully satisfied, and loaden with all the Graces and Bounties, good Subjects could hope to receive upon such an Address to their Prince; and what needed Confirmation in Parliament, was to be done when the Parliament should meet, at the day to which it was Prorogued. The People of *Ireland* were never better pleased then with the gracious Returns his Majesty had made by their Commissioners. That Kingdom never enjoyed a more profound, and more like to be lasting Peace and Prosperity, Commerce and Trade, both at home and abroad, never flourished more;

barbarous

barbarous Customs were never more entirely subdued and abrogated; there never was more Unity, Friendship, and good Agreement, amongst all sorts and degrees (except in the standing root of mischief, the difference in Religion) then at this time, nor more mutual Confidence. I can say, being that time there, the Sheep and the Goats lived quietly together; and there was that intire trust in one another, as to all Matters Civil and Temporal, that I remember very well, the Summer before the Rebellion, The Titular Bishop of *Fernes* coming his Visitation into the County of *Wexford*, where I then dwelt, at the request of a Popish Priest, I lent most of my Silver Plate to entertain the said Bishop with, and had it honestly restored. In this serene and happy state was that Kingdom, every one sitting under his own Vine and Fig-tree in peace, and in the abundance of all things, when, whether surfeiting of Quiet and Plenty,

C or

or by the just Judgment of God upon a sinful and superstitious Nation; or that the said Committees having staid in *England* till they saw symptoms of a misunderstanding between his Majesty and his two Houses of Parliament in *England*, and being most of them Papists, conceived they had fallen into a fit juncture to set up their darling Idolatry, and restore the pretended Jurisdiction of their Idolized Forraign Power of the Pope of *Rome*, or being in at the Intrigues of the Popish Faction all Court, and receiving incouragement by what they observed, and was infused into them; they had here laid the Foundation of the Massacre and Rebellion, whereof *Ireland* was to be the Scene; or upon what other grounds, I shall not here take upon me determine, but I well remember that he 23d. of *October*, after their Return, broke out upon a formed Combination and Conspiracy, wherein almost all the said Popish Committees were

leading

leading Men and principal Actors, such a horrid and bloody Massacre and Rebellion, as is not to be parallell'd in History; neither Man, Woman, nor Infants in the Womb, or at the Breast, being spared; but the generality of that Nation turning barbarous and wild *Irish* again, after so many hundred years Subjection to the Crown of *England*, and Endeavours of their Reformation and Civilizing to so vast an expence of Blood and Treasure, as is hardly to be believed. But, my Lord, I may now but touch at things, *Comme en passant*, that I may keep within the bounds of a *Letter*; but when, what I have meditated, and am preparing from Records and authentick, unquestionble Relations and Transactions of that bloody Tragedy and matchless Defection from the Crown and very Nation of *English* Men, shall see the light, your Lordship will be informed, of what, it seems, hath not yet come to your know-

knowledge, and what must make your Lordship blush, at your so fatal mistake, to have ever been (so far (as you confess your self) in so ill Company, and to have partaken in the least in so foul a Guilt.

Having made this necessary Excursion and Caution, I proceed in your Lordships own Method, Going first with your Lordship to the Lords Justices, acquainting them of your willingness to serve the King against the Rebels, to which no doubt, by advice of his Majesties Privy Council in that Kingdom, they gave a very prudent Answer, That your Religion was an obstacle; and how could they well say less, when it was apparent that it was a Popish Conspiracy, and those of that profession universally ingaged in the Defection; in so much that though the State there would have distinguished them into Allegiance, and for that end, more out of desire to win them than any confidence they had in them, but
to

to leave them without excuse, put Arms and Ammuuition into the hands of the Lord Viscount *Gormanston*; and other Popish Lords and Gentlemen of best Quality and Estates in the English Pale; and who by their tenures had formerly, and were obliged to assist the Crown, in times of danger; and they, almost all of them, went with his Majesties Arms in Aid of the Rebells; and they who did best, did but restore the Kings Arms, and joyned themselves, and all the power they could make, to the Insurrection; forgetting the Grants and bountiful Gifts of Lands their Ancestors had received from the Crown, for former, and on condition of future Service; in which Rank your Lordship placeth your noble Ancestors, and I heartily wish you had continued that station.

Your Lordships next motion was to the Lords Justices, for a Pass to go for *England*, which, though they could not

not consent to, they gave your Lordship good Advice, and which for a time you followed (*viz.*) to go home to your House, being but 20 miles from *Dublin*, and under the protection or reach of the State, as there should be occasion, and as your Lordship found afterwards.

Concerning your Lordships entertaining my Lord of *Antrim* and the Dutchess of *Buckingham* at *Madinstowne*, whither they soon followed, whither by consent with your Lordship is not said, and your delight in their company, I have nothing to say, but that it was an ill time for Feasting and Jollity, when stript, and almost starved *English*, came flying by your Gate every day from the Rebels Cruelty. And I find, that both the Marquess of *Antrim* and the Dutchess, were after that deeply ingaged in the Rebellion; and her Grace living and dying in the *Irish* Quarters, chose to be buried at *Waterford*. And though your

your Lordship had power enough, when the *Irish* came and drove away a great part of your Stock; to recover it, by a party sent out with your Brother, who brought with him two or three of the chiefest Conductors of that Rabble; yet you do not so much as pretend that you delivered up any of them to Justice (as you ought.) But you say that this inraged the *Irish* so much, as you conceived your Brother was not safe there (where yet you thought fit to continue; but sending him to *Dublin* to attend the Justices Orders, and assure them of your readiness to return on a Call, they sending a Convoy, which they promised to do as occasion required, yet your Lordship hearing that you were indicted of high Treason (the most publick way of accusing, though your Brothers Letter calls it Clandestine) you went to *Dublin* (it seems you could go when you pleased without a Convoy) but did not, it seems, think fit to appaer and oppose the Indictment, but being committed by the Lords Justices and Council (the Justification whereof is not the work of this Letter, but will have its proper time and place) your Lordship after addressing your Case, by your Brother, to the King and Parliament in *England*, without success, whither your Brother, being refused a Pass by the Justices, was gotten. It seems your Lordship meditated your escape into the *Irish* Quarters, and relate the manner how you compassed the same, which few will believe your Lordship would have done, or held it the way to save your self, but that you knew you had deserved it of them, and that they had no cause to hurt you, as appeared after, by their making you General of their Horse; and your Lordship, chusing the Oath of Association before that of Allegiance.

Your Lordships having now shifted sides, betake your self roundly to a justification of the Rebels cause, I must follow

follow you your own way, though it be not so methodical as I could wish, and is with great confusion of times and affairs, which the thred of History will reduce to order when time serves. It is true, that Parties were sent out by the Justices, according to his Majesties Direction, to kill and destroy the Rebels throughout all the parts of the Kingdom; and if the Officers and Souldiers did not take care enough (in your Lordships Opinion) to distinguish between the Rebels and the Subjects, but killed in many places promiscuously (whereof your Lordship gives no instances, or of particular complaints to have been made of any such thing) I would fain know what distinction could be made of those that were found in Arms or Action against the Kings Authority; for there will appear to have been no prosecution of others, nor any others killed, unless by such accidents as might happen in full peace, and when the course of Justice is free. But

But your Lordship faith, that on this partly, and partly on other occasions that preceded, and some too that followed (but you enumerate none) the whole Nation finding themselves concerned, took Arms for their own defence; and particularly the Lords of the Pale did so, who yet at the same time, desired the Justices to send their Petition to the King, which was refused.

This being the chief ground by which your Lordship would justifie the most formed and dangerous Conspiracy and Rebellion that ever was in that Kingdom since the Crown of *Englands* first Title thereunto, which your Lordship (being a Peer of *England*) should have distinguished from a just and a lawful War, but do not. I must observe to your Lordship, that its an ill way to acquaint the King with their pretended Grievances, *La main a lespe;* they should have done that, if they had any, before their treache-

treacherous and bloody Massacres and open Rebellion; but indeed they had none to offer, but what was the just return of their own black Actions; for your Lordship knows (as I have said before) that by Committees of both Houses of Parliament in *Ireland*, whereof most were Papists, they had just before their Rebellion, returned loaden with such Graces and Condescentions of Favour from the Crown, as had been sufficient (meeting with the least ingenuity, gratitude and humanity) to have made wavering Persons good Subjects; but the Lord *Macguires* and others Confessions, manifested that they had laid their Design of Treason too deep to retreat easily, when they had once struck the stroak, till finding their error, not from remorse, but from sense of danger imminent (which must inevitably follow, unless they could subdue *England* too. At the first they made a loud cry of Grievances, and at length bid fair, as they

they had made *Ireland* a field of Blood and Defolation, to difturb *England* alfo.

Concerning the further difcouragement the Rebels received by Sir *John Reads* treatment, and what that was, and upon what grounds, though I have all the paffages thereof by me, and will by no means allow of Racking any Man, as being contrary to the Law of *England*; yet I muft obferve that it was a very jealous time, after fo many thoufands flaughtered barbaroufly in cold blood, the Rebellion increafing every day, too great a curiofity arifing to know the bottom of the defign, that remedies proportionable might be applied; and Sir *John Read* being one of the Kings Servants and a defigning Papift, being there fo unfeafonably, without being able to give a good account of himfelf or bufinefs, and going away Agent for the Rebels in Arms, without leave of the State, might make them exceed the ftrict bounds

bounds of Law in his Examination

Your Lordship in the next place taking notice that you had tryed this and other ways to acquaint the King with your Grievances (which I have shewed before were none) and all failing, an open War broke forth generally throughout the Kingdom; this being a meer colour and pretence, your Lordship unfortunately puts the effect before the pretended cause; for by what you had said before, and what the truth of the cause is, the horrid Rebellion, (for it never merited the name of a War) was universal, before they so much as alleadged any Grievance. Your next *Memoire* is of your entertaining my Lord of *Ormond* at Dinner after the Battle of *Kilrush*, which you were a Spectator of; and that some who came with him, turned it another way, publishing through the Army that it was a Feast for my Lord *Mountgarret* and the Rebels, which through the *English* Quarters past for currant.

Here

Here your Lordship, by your own shewing, intimates, that though you were a Spectator from your own House of a Battle, wherein the Crown lay at stake, and had formerly discovered you had force enough to recover your Cattel taken away by the Rebels, and apprehend some of their Leaders, which you call Rogues, yet (though a Peer of both Kingdoms) you would be no Actor, though the Kings General was at your Gate, doubting, it seems, the event of Battle; but the success rendring my Lord of *Ormond* Victorious, you set before him that Dinner, which you had not strength to keep from him. And indeed it was generally then held by the *English*, that if the Rebels had gained the day, your Lordship would more frankly have bid the Lord *Mountgarret*, their General (and a *Butler* also) welcome to that Dinner than you did my Lord of *Ormond*; and this is what passeth rant in this particular to this day, which you

you believe was much the cauſe of that villainous proceeding (as you call it) fore-mentioned, whereas it ſeems you were ſo far from being ill dealt with in the leaſt, that my Lord of *Ormond*, your Gueſt, though he might have juſtified his carrying you Priſoner with him to *Dublin*, who would not aſſiſt him in Fight, as your Tenure required left you (as ſome think by a blameable omiſſion) Maſter of your own Houſe, and without the leaſt damage done you, though much happened after to the Kingdom by your liberty, of which you were for ſome time reſtrained in the Sheriffs hands, and after ordered to be removed to the Caſtle of *Dublin*, which you ſay ſtartled you, and it brought to your thoughts the proceedings againſt the Earl of *Strafford*, &c. whereupon you made an eſcape, probably in the manner related.

But here your Lordſhip, not diſtinguiſhing times, and I not having Papers

pers by me, am so doubtful of an intermixture of Affairs to your advantage, that I must reserve the unfolding thereof to another tſme, when I shall be able exactly to shew you the times of your Lordships appearing and joyning with the Rebels; and of the proceeding against the Earl of *Strafford*, and how they preceded on the other. I shall only for the present, observe how that great personage (though more innocent than your Lordship could pretend to) never fled his Tryal, well knowing that would have fixed more guilt upon him in construction of Law, than could be proved against him; and judged it more honourable to hazard the losing of his Head than his Innocency. Your Lordships Wisdom took a contrary course, and concluding that Innocency was a scurvy plea in an angry time (as indeed it is in any times, where it is so thin laid, that gross guilt appears under it) you find it safer to arraign the
state

state than to abide a Tryal; and accordingly taxing them for passion and partiality, and to be of the Parliaments perswasion (when your Lordship would have had them and the whole Kingdom of yours, and by what means time hath manifested) you resolved to attempt an escape and save your self in the *Irish* Quarters, which your Lordship did to the Mountains of *Wicklow*; where being come, you cared little for the Justices. Is it possible, if your Lordship had thought your self innocent, that you would seek safety, or count your self safe among the most enormously bloody and guilty men that ever were under the Sun; and fly the Kings Justice with reflection and scorn upon the State, that was pursuing them for their Crimes; and to avoid the inward stings of Guilt or Apprehensions of Punishment, run head-long into open and avowed Guilt, among those who were under Gods Vengeance and the Kings. I leave this to your Lordships more serious second thoughts.

Being out of the danger of Justice, though your Lordship cared little for the Justices (as how could your Lordship, when you were associated with those who had bid defiance to God and the King) yet your Lordship quickly saw a proof, how civil and merciful they had been to you hitherto, when they upon your escape, shewed you they had power enough to pursue you, and pillage and burn your House in your Mountain view, and use your Family as Enemies, which they might have done before, but their constant course was to endeavour the re-gaining those who had faltered in their Allegiance, and not to increase the number, which was too heavy upon them already.

Your Lordship at length arrived to the beloved place designed, the City of *Kilkenny*, head Quarters of the Confederate Rebels, where you found many

many of your acquaintance preparing for their natural defence, seeing no distinction made, or safety but in Arms.

Your Lordships heart was now at rest among your Friends and Relations, to whom indeed, after committing all the wickedness their hand of violence could reach to, being defeated in several Battels by his Majesties Forces, and driven into their holds, defence became nutural, their Crimes having left them no hopes but in Arms, and who could expect no distinction to be made, wehre they were universally involved in the same black guilt.

For this end your Lordship saith they had chosen a Counil, formed an Oath of Association, made Four Generals of the Four Provinces, caused a Seal to be made, raised Monies, constituted a General Assembly, &c. all ensigns of the more than regal Power they had usurped. To this Council your Lordship was sent for, and being well prepared by those inclinations which made you forsake the Kings Government and the Laws, you quickly closed with them upon the grounds before expressed, and upon consideration of their model of Government, and very reasonable (as your Lordship judged it) Oath of Association, which your Lordship prints at large, and their desiring your conjunction, with thanks returned, your Lordship engaged your self to run a Fortune with them, upon very ill principles, if anger and revenge inclined you to it as much as any other consideration (which you intimate, though you say you cannot resolve.)

Its strange how the Earl of *Castlehaven* and Lord *Audley* in *England* could close so cordially with the *Irish*, who had shed so much innocent *English* Blood in full peace, and think himself justified by such an account of his ingagement as this, unless he had been resolved in the justice of their cause

cause from the beginning, however he carried it with seeming fairness to the Lords Justices till he got out of their reach.

But ingaged your Lordship was, and being thus Confederate, and having taken the Oath of Association, becoming one of their Council, and General of the Horse under *Preston*, and giving the most specious account you can of your proceedings in that quality. Truth being the greatest and best friend, I had rather one or several Persons and Families, should lie under the Consequences of its impartiality, than that the *English* Nation and Protestant Religion should suffer by a timorous unworthy concealing, or withholding any part of it. And since your Lordship, to palliate or justifie your own Actions, and the Confederate *Irish* Cause, endeavours to render the generality of the *English* Protestants Criminal, your Lordship must not think it much, that I, one of *English* Race, and

and for Religion of the Church of *England*, should be a little plain in their Justification and Defence; and for that end remove the mask your Lordship hath put upon the face of Affairs, by continuing my Remarques upon your Lordships Memoires. And first to the constitution of a Council, it was made up of Members uncapable of that trust by Law. In the Oath of Association, and Propositions grounded thereon, there is not a word but breaths high Treason (except the first thirteen lines, which set up the Kings Name and Authority only in pagentry and mockery, to be crucified and contradicted by all that follows; and yet this Oath your Lordship held very reasonable, as the case then stood, that is, when you and your Confederates were incouraged or heightned with a Power able, as you fancied, to make good what you had sworn. And suitable to this ungodly, trayterous Oath, were all the subsequent proceedings of the Confedefederates, their Councils at home and their Actions abroad, their Cessations and pretended Peaces, which I shall take notice of more particularly in their respective series of time.

The general Assembly met the 24th of *October* 1642; your Lordship saith it differ'd nothing from a Parliament, but that the Lords and Commons sate together, and not in two Houses. Was this so inconsiderable a difference in the Opinion of a Peer of *England* as well as *Ireland*, or fit for one of so noble Extraction to be submitted to, against Honour, Law and right Reason. But the truth is, and I speak it for the honour of the Nobility of *Ireland*, the Rebels had not debauched enough of them, either for interest or number, to bear the Countenance of a House of Peers, or to be of any considerable figure among that People, who having cast off Majesty could not be warmed by the beams thereof, which I count the Nobility; but they resolved of course

course into common persons again, and had but single Votes among the Croud, instead of those Honourable Priviledges and Negative Voice, which their Ancestors had acquired as the just reward of their faithfulness to the Crown in former times, and in all Defections and Rebellions since the subjection of that Nation to *England*. And this your Lordship ingeniously confesseth (and faith we see it) was a force-put upon you, and you hoped in time the storm being passed, to return to your old Government under the King. Here you own the being fallen from it, but could your Lordship imagine, or any others believe, this Cob-web pretence possible, were you not all ingaged by the bond of an Oath to the contrary, and to preserve your new upstart treasonable Model and Constitution; and that the storm should never cease till you had by Arms attained a confirmation of all that you had done, for which, by the said Oath, you

you renounced the receiving any Pardon or Protection, but by your own Sword. But that Assembly differed also from a Parliament in this, That it was called by a packt party of bloody Papists in Rebellion and Confederacy, and had neither Legal nor Regal Authority.

But to conciliate, credit and belief, you add, That there were many learned in the Law amongst you, whom you incouraged to keep you as near the old Government as might be, holding to the Ancient Laws of the Land.

This is as improbable as the other, but if true, is a demonstration that *Irish* Popish Lawyers, are the worst instruments that can be tollerated in *Ireland*. And it is notorious in Fact, that these were the Men that did both contrive and put in order the Rebellion, and frame their whole Constitution, and without whose Council and Abilities (having had their Education in the Inns of Court of *England*) they

they had never come out of that Chaos of Confusion, where they were at first, or reduced their Affairs to a consistency, but had been quickly mastered. And therefore I hope this hint concerning the Lawyers will awaken his Majesty and Parliament of *England*, and the Government in *Ireland*, to provide against the continuance of such dangerous instruments, as the Popish Lawyers have shewed themselves to be, and in probability will so continue, making use of their Learning and Skill for subversion of Government and good Order. So that *Ireland* is never like to be quiet if they be tollerated. Your Lordship proceeds to tell us, that this Assembly without delay approved all the Council had done, (how could they well in gratitude do less, being themselves a Creature of that Councils making) and settled a Model of Government, *viz*. That at the end of every General Assembly, the supream Council should be confirmed

ed or changed, as they thought fit. That it should consist of Twenty five, six out of each Province, three of the six still resident, the 25th was your Lordship, with no relation to any Province, but to the Kingdom in general, &c. Your Lordships Relation was a mock Image of his Majesty, which was also to the Kingdom in general, and but that it is not now my business, I could here evince that this Constitution cast the over balance of the Government clearly into the *Irish* hands, such of the old *English* Extraction as joyned with them, being Ciphers upon the matter, as it appeared afterwards in practice. So improbable was what your Lordship asserts, that if a Letter came to them written in *Irish*, it would be wondred at, and hardly could one be found to read it, unless you would confess, that those skilled in reading the *Irish* Language are extinct; for the meerest *Irish* of that Kingdom, and all the Popish

pish Clergy, who (if any) are likl‑est to be skilled in it, were ingaged in the Rebellion, and constant promoters of it, having their Colledges and Monasteries in *Kilkenny*, and all Cities and chief Towns under the Confederate *Irish* Power, and wholly at their Command. For a close of this Paragraph, your Lordship saith, you were not in case to bring to Justice those that begun the Rebellion, but you never saw any of them esteemed or advanced. This is strange, when *Owen Roe Oneal*, Sir *Phelemy Oneal*, *Con Oneal*, the Mc. *Donnels*, Mc. *Thomas*, the *Farrolls*, the *Delyes*, the Mc. *Cartyes*, Mc. *Guires*, Mc. *Mahans*, *Fitzpatricks*, Mc. *Gennis's*; and generally those of the meer *Irish* septs and Families, were chiefly trusted, whose names it were too tedious to repeat, but I have Authentick Lists of them; but indeed I do believe the Confederates, even of *English* Extraction, had as little will as power to question those that

that begun the Rebellion; and to this day they are so far from any inclination to condemn it, that all their Writings run in Justification of it; and I never yet met with any that cordially seemed to repent it, or perswade others to it, except only *Peter Walsh*, whom your Lordship calls your Ghostly Father *Caron*, and some few Remonstrants with them, who condemning the Doctrines of Rebellion, King killing, and Deposing, &c. do obliquely censure this Rebellion; and some of them positively call the beginners and continuers thereof to repentance.

The rest of your Lordships *Memoires* is more History than Justification, as well whilst you continued to serve under the Confederate Catholicks, which was till the Peace of 1646, proclaimed, as after, till you left *Ireland*, wherein your Lordships part being mixed of Gallentry and Generosity in some instances, as well as Severity and fierce Prosecution of the *English*

English in others. I will not be a critical obferver thereof, or lead any to envy your Lordſhip, the juſt eſteem of whatever you did honourably, though in an ill cauſe. But ſince your Lordſhip lays ſome weight of merit upon the Ceſſation, and two Peaces of 1646, and 1648, and expreſſeth no unfavourable Opinion of that which goes by the name of *Glamorgan*'s Peace, and think much that the *Iriſh* their Eſtates were given away by the Acts of Settlement. I ſhall only make ſome general Remarks upon thoſe particulars, and the whole ſtate of that Rebellion, and ſo put an end to your Lordſhips trouble and my own.

And firſt, I muſt obſerve upon the whole matter, that the *Iriſh* did the *Engliſh* more hurt, and advantage themſelves more by the Ceſſation and two firſt Peaces, than ever they did or could do by open force after the firſt Maſſacre, upon this grounds, the Lords Jvſtices and Council, were from the

the beginning averse to them; and for me to shew the Design and Intrigue of the Cessation and Peaces, which I can do by unquestionable Memorials and Records, will make a great part of a volumn, and cannot well come within the bounds of a Letter; but when I have said all, I think fit to your Lordship, upon occasion of your Letter, your Lordship, who as you were an Enemy, as keen as generous) having been by your place and interest privy to all the Cabals and secret Councils against the *English* and *Protestants*, being deeply ingaged in the Roman Catholick Confederacy; and any other Attempts against them, in what shape or form soever they appeared) will I hope, if you find any thing written by me questionable or doubtful in your opinion, favour me with your severest Reflections thereupon; for as I design nothing but exact truth wherever it light, so if by inadvertincy or want of full information,

I

I should erre, or come short in the least, your Lordship shall find me ready to retract or supply, but never to persist in it.

Your Lordship knows as well as any man, that the Earl of *Ormond*, made afterwards Marquess and Duke with the same Title, was the first of that Family of the *Botelers*, that was Educated in the Protestant Religion; his Mother the Lady *Thurles*, Brothers, Sisters, and all his Relations continuing Roman Catholicks, and in the Irish Quarters, and those able to bear Arms, as the Lord *Muskery*, after Earl of *Clancarty*, and Collonel *Fitzpatrick*, his Brother in Law, his Brother Collonel *Richard Butler* of *Kilcash*, and Collonel *George Mathewes*, and other his Relations; as the Lords *Mountgarret*, *Dunboyne*, and divers other Lords, and others of his Name and Family, were Generals or Commanders of lower Quality in the Rebels Army; so that his Lordship was upon the matter single
in

in any Duty and Allegiance to the Crown; all his Lordſhips Friends, Kindred and Dependants, taking the contrary part; and his Lordſhip eſcaping ſoon after the Rebellion to *Dublin*, only with the Kings Troop, which he Commanded, and ſome Servants that attended him. The Earl of *Leiceſter*, Lord Lieutenant, as he was upon his Journey for *Ireland*, was diſcharged that Imployment, to make way for the Marqueſs of *Ormond* to ſucceed him, who had an unlimitted Commiſſion ſent him, ſole to examine the pretended Grievances of the *Iriſh*, and for making a Ceſſation with the Rebels, which he did, and was after made Lord Lieutenant, and concluded the two firſt Peaces before mentioned. I have heard Sir *Philip Percival*, a very worthy Perſon and of a fair Eſtate, being asked why he would by his Certificates of Defect of Stores, give countenance and furtherance to a Ceſſation, which he he knew could only advantage the Rebels, and be ruinous to the *English*? Anſwer, The Stores were really waſted upon unprofitable, fruitleſs Marches, and then his Certificates being required, he durſt not (as an Officer) refuſe them, though he was aware of the uſe would be made of them.

To ſhew your Lordſhip how the Ceſſation operated (laying aſide at preſent, the queſtion of the warrantableneſs on neceſſity thereof) and that the two firſt Peaces were againſt Law, and ſeveral Acts of Parliament, in both Kingdoms (and upon that and other accounts, the validity thereof) I muſt take another opportunity, when I may diſcourſe things more fully with your Lordſhip. I can now only briefly tell your Lordſhip, that all the Proceedings of the Rebels in Arms, and all their Demands, were Treaſon: That the *Engliſh* and Proteſtants had the Laws on their ſide, which the *Iriſh* by combination

bination and force did break, and designed wholly to subvert: That the *Irish* tollerated no Protestants in their Quarters, though that Religion were the only legal Establishment; but seized and forfeited all their Estates, whilst the Protestants afforded the measure and benefit of the Laws to the *Irish* and Papists, even to those who had been in Rebellion, whensoever they came in or submitted.

It is not then to be wondred at, that the chief and most of the *English* Nobility in *Ireland*, and the generality of *English*, *Scotch*, and *Irish* Protestants of all qualities and degrees, sooner or later, opposed both the Cessation and Peaces, as destructive to them, and derogatory to the Crown, in which number we find, the Earls of *Kildare*, *Thomond*, *Cork*, *Barrimore*, *Drogheda*, *Donnagall*, *Claubrasill*, *Mount Alexander*, &c. The Viscounts of *Valentia*, *Conoway*, *Ranelagh*, *Kinnelmeky*,

nelmeky, Shannon, &c. Barons or Lords Elsmond Juchequin, Blaney, Broghill, &c. But it were endless to name all, and of no use to your Lordship, who know this as well as I.

By this it appears how ungratefully the Irish did requite the Marquess of Ormond, for his unwillingness that the whole Irish Nation should ruin themselves by their persisting in Rebellion. And now, whether it was their vain confidence to carry the day, or what else occasioned it, they lost the opportunity of deliverance, which the Marquess of Ormond being related to so many of them by Blood and Alliance, had compassionately designed for them, though with great hardship and damage to the English. And whatever grounds the Marquess of Ormond had for the Cessation and Peaces (by which he could have got nothing, but would have incurred manifest loss) which it chiefly concerns himself to vouch,
that

that in the eye of the World he may stand clear, as a true *English* Man and faithful Subject. It is apparent, that now by the Forfeiture and Punishment of the *Irish*, his Lordship and Family are the greatest gainers of the Kingdom, and have added to their Inheritances vast scopes of Land, and a Revenue three times greater than what his Paternal Estate was before the Rebellion; and most of his increase is out of their Estates who adheared to the Peaces, or served under his Majesties Ensigns abroad; which shews, that whatsoever of Compassion or Natural Affection, or otherwise, might incline him to make those Peaces, he is in Judgment and Conscience against them, and so hath since appeared, and hath advantage by their laying aside. The like may be said of the Duke of *York*, the Earl of *Arlington*, Lord *Lanesborough*, and others, who have great Estates of the *Irish* freely given them upon the same foundation. So that 'tis to be hoped whether the Bills already come over to confirm the forfeited Rebels Estates to *English* and Protestants, will do the work or no. That his Grace, or whosoever shall succeed him in the Lieutenancy, will in time transmit such Bills as shall do that work effectually, and unite and strengthen his Majesties Protestant Subjects, to oppose and break the further Designs of that Rebellious Generation, which they will never keep free from, so long as they acknowledge and obey a Forreign Head.

I shall make no reflection at this time upon the Peace called *Glamorgan*'s Peace, but what your Lordship gives occasion for by mentioning it, *viz.* That it was the most destructive of all to the *English* and Protestants, but suited best with the Confederate Design of establishing the *Romish* Idolatry, which your Lordship in your Oath of Associ-

Affociation engaged as deep in as any, excepting the firſt foundation laid in Blood, a fit baſis for a Faction, only ſupported by Fraud and Cruelty.

One paſſage in your Lordſhips *Memoires* I cannot but take notice of, for your Honour, as an *Engliſh* Man, That when the Marques of *Ormond* in his extremity, between the Nuncio party and the Parliament of *England*, asked your Lordſhip with which of his Enemies he ſhould treat. You anſwered, That you were confident he had reſolved that before, there being no queſtion in the caſe; when it was no queſtion with your Lordſhip, I wonder how it came to be one with his Lordſhip; but the ſucceſs of your Council was happy, and founded upon ſolid grounds of Reaſon.

Your Lordſhip ſees I can but glance at particulars in this Letter, and being (by ſo noble a Pens ingaging in juſtification of a Quarrel, which caſts reflection

ction upon all that took contrary part to the *Irish*, of which number I was one) contrary to my first intention upon the matter, necessitated (in vindication of as just a cause as ever was managed under the Sun) to hasten out the last part of the general History of *Ireland* first (Wherein I shall so impartially make relation beyond all possibility of contradiction, that I doubt not your Lordship will reflect with remorse upon what you have done and written, wherein I differ from you, and the World will know exactly the truth of that sad story.) I shall in the mean time, only as in an abstract, set these things before you, and upon the whole matter in answer to your Lordships specious justification, and for your present mortification, let you know that by Judgment of the King and his Privy Councils and Parliaments in both Kingdoms. You are involved in the guilt of Treason, and under forfeiture

feiture of all you have, and as a friend, yet advise you to get his Majesties Pardon, if the Acts of Parliaments have not precluded you; for itsmore than I know if all your Lordships active Services in *Ireland* be not yet liable to the utmost penalties and Severities of the Law. So far are they from being fit to be offered as entertainment to his Majesty by an Epistle Dedicatory, as your Lordship hath done.

I find your Lordship in several places reflects upon those who broke the first Peace, and call it unparallell'd breach of Faith, punished by heavy Judgments from Heaven; and yet this was the Confederates own Act. But as if the breach of the Oath of Allegiance by the *Irish*, and their treacherous and bloody defection from the Crown of *England*, were a Peccadillo, your Lordship hardly takes notice of it, but repines at the forfeiture of Estates grounded thereupon, though God and Man agreed in that Vengeance and Punishment. And

And let this Rebellion be compared to all before it, there will not appear, since the *English* Title to *Ireland*, so just and clear grounds of forfeiture and extirpating a Nation, as have done upon this; but the King hath mingled Mercy with Justice; and though by a Providence from Heaven to the *English*, the Marquesses of *Ormond* and *Clanrickard*, his Majesties chief Governors, incouraged the *Irish* to keep up a War against the *English*, wherein they were so much hardened to their ruin, that they were at length intirely subdued, without condition to any save for life, and left to be as miserable as they had made others in all other respects, yet multitudes of them have been restored, and must yet own their Lives and Estates to the Clemency of the King, and the mildness of the *English* Government, which they had cast off, and put themselves under a Forreign Yoke, which neither we nor our Fathers

thers were able to bear. The Wisdom of God thus punishing one sin of theirs with another, till they are scarce a People; and the *English* and Protestant interest never more flourishing in that Kingdom. Insomuch, that it would be now the greatest folly imaginable in the Government of *England* and *Ireland*, ever to suffer the *Papists* to grow capable of raising such a Rebellion again, which they will certainly do when able; Bigottery and sottish Ignorance, both of Priests and People in Religion, being the growing root of mischief there.

Upon the whole, since the Cobweb excuses your Lordship hath made, cannot cover the Blood that hath been shed, or bring quiet to the Consciences of any that had hand therein; and since your Lordship so well knows the Temper and Constitution of the *Irish*, by your long continuance and interest among them, I cannot but yet hope and

and therefore do with the most friendly adjurations beseech your Lordship herein) that the zeal, which you yet seem to have for the King his Laws, and the *English* Government, will incline you to let him know (the truth you cannot be ignorant of) that they are a Nation never to be trusted till reformed, that so his Majesty and his *English* Subjects may run no more hazards of suffering by confidence in them, or regard to their *Crocodile* Tears and groundless Complaints, by which they have deceived the *English* in all times. And that by your Repentance, imitating your Ghostly Father *Peter Walsh*, his Advice to his Countrey Men for Repentance and change of Principles, your Lordship may give another instance to the World that Allegiance and the Religion you profess may dwell in the same Breast, then which nothing can more conduce to divert the *Irish* from future Attempts of Rebellion. My

My Lord, I find many Queries fit to be made on your *Memoires*, and many other particulars; a *Redire* therein, but you will, perhaps, think I have done too much already. I shall therefore reserve these to another opportunity, and here close in the wonted manner, with the assurance of my being (saving in the *Irish* Confederacy and Matter of Religion)

My Lord,

 Your Lordships

  Affectionate Friend

   and Servant.

POST-

Postscript.

THis Letter *was written, as appears, in* August 1680, *presently after the Earl of* CASTLEHAVEN *had Published his Memoires, with a Dedication only to the King; but since his Lordships Receipt of this Letter, he was, it seems, convinced of the necessity of writing the* Epistle to the Reader, *in Condemnation of the* Irish *Rebellion, which his Lordship hath since caused to be Printed, with the said Memoires.*

FINIS.

SOC
DA
943
C3
1974

DATE DUE